CW00521610

My Time of Life

Essays of Footprints

Anthony Shillingford

These memoirs are dedicated to all my grandchildren

Contents

CHAPTER 1

"Walk with Kings....." "If" from Poems by Rudyard Kipling

On the last day of June in 2007, two septuagenarians were leaving the royal apartments at Windsor Castle after a commemoration dinner. "How do we come to be here?" they marvelled, chuckling cheerfully as they went out into the late summer night.

It was over 65 years since we had been there, and many of the faces and people whom we remembered had been and gone. We could recall afternoons spent singing with the family, a tea party in the Red Drawing Room, where now hang the portraits by Sir Gerald Kelly, which we had observed in the painting and touched the robes. We had even seen seen a pantomime at Christmas where the sisters excelled in Bing Crosby numbers. We had the privilege of seeing that family, not a large family in private and in the environment which they enjoyed, away from the glare of publicity which engulfed their lives both then, in time of war and would do in the future. The place, Windsor Castle their home, would still be the same and generations after us would still be a part of it. At this time in the war they were, as others have said, hospitable and open people with time to spare, and laughter to share as, like us, they were growing up.

My friend Tony and I could laugh and talk about those days and see it all vividly. We were privileged, as we were when we both arrived at King's College Cambridge, to complete our formal education. We were again benefitting from royal benevolence, King's being another royal foundation, set up for ordinary people like us, who just happened by good luck to be there and privileged to be a part of it.

Perhaps now is the time to set my story down and put some of it on record. It is both social history, and, perhaps for me, a time to bring up those sins of comission and omission in a life which had been full and varied. "Time for amendment of life" as the Book of Common Prayer has it. Charles Dickens wrote memories "come back to me in music, in the wind, in the dead stillness of the night, in revolving years"[1]. Exploring memory, recalling and setting it down, is the basis of all autobiography.

In a recently prepared memoir of my grandfather, I had been able to read his political speeches and to understand the surrounding debates, in which they were made. It had a sense of those times which fascinated me. We are not all politicians, so we do not have that daily record, available at libraries, but perhaps my own grandchildren may one day be interested to read what I now write, and as Alan Bennett has put it "Pass the parcel. That's sometimes all you can do. Take it, feel it and pass it on. Not for me, not for you, but for someone, somewhere, one day."[2] "To walk with Kings" was uplifting and spoiling, to say the least, but I also saw the other side of the coin, declining industries in Belfast, the demise of coal and the hopelessness in Bangladesh and Nepal. It was important "to keep the common touch." Yet through it all I met and mixed with others who like me were not deterred from doing what we had to d, and carrying on. Through it all I learnt to respect and like people and to enjoy the company of those, with whom one either worked with or came across; the wretched as well as the successful; those who never saw more than their districts and those who travelled the globe; the idealists and those set in their ways. There are very few that I would not want to meet again and many whose memories I cherish. Most had a sense of humour and a sense of the ridiculous; some became ill and died under strain and stress; there were plenty of accidents to shock and disturb. To finish with Kipling "Yours is the world and everything that's in it" You should never be frightened but go for it." Or as St Paul told the Phillippians "Press on."

If I write about people it is not gossip. Suzanne says that we Irish go on talking about people until we find out that the person in question is related or a "connection." If I write about things it is because I recall them still and that they interest me. J.F Kennedy said "I am an idealist without illusions."[3] If you achieve something it is written about elsewhere. Reports about me are few and most press cuttings including one in "Private Eye" are not worth recording. Most letters of gratitude, which I have received relate only to an occasion which I may describe elsewhere in this memoir. To mix among interesting characters and human beings is about being part of the "music of a time" as someone once said, and it amuses because the social ways of today are different from those of the past.

My advice for others is not to be cast down, don't bear resentment, keep going and enjoy the fun of life. "Keep that which is committed to you" is a remembered text from my confirmation. There is plenty to find and to recall. In this my eighth decade I can still pause and remember, dream and smile, perhaps even regret a little, it would not be human not to do so, but I never wish to forget, and I hope that I can continue as I am for some time. As my eldest grandchildren Jack and Eve reach their twentieth year and embark on their own lives in the twenty first century, along with their younger cousins, it is something to pass on to them and to show them, as in the same Kipling poem, how to "To meet with triumph and disaster, and treat those two imposters just the same."

This is an attempt to put on record, for a large and growing family, what I can still recall, some of which may seem strange to them, as it now passes into history. Some of us, at my stage of life, feel the urge to chronicle, and my cousins and I, when we meet, often laugh and encourage each other as we remember those who were around when we were growing up. On reflection we come to understand them better.

The form of this memoir, "My time of life," will be to write each chapter as it happened chronologically, but included are essays not only about a time but a continuing interest. This is about those, whom I have met along the road. It is now time to pull back the curtain and begin the play of life.

[1] *Charles Dickens by Peter Ackroyd* [2] *The History Boys by Alan Bennett* [3]*John F.Kennedy, President United States*

CHAPTER 2

Beginnings

Ulster or the six counties of Northern Ireland was where I was brought up in the early 1930s. I was the offspring of a Shillingford with a Shillington, the latter being a family in trade and politics, in that community. My parents met when Tony, my father had been at Worcester College Oxford at the same time as Maurice Shillington, my mother Mabel's cousin. They got to know each other because of mix ups with mail. Mabel was at Headington School, and she used to visit the College. Tony became an education officer in northern Nigeria, a place which I was to visit, when older, but for the time being I was to be based in Belfast at Mabel's family home Strandtown . Do and Mo, my grandparents were to be the centre of my life. Mabel, aged 24 at my birth, was a history graduate, as was Tony. Whether I was unexpected I shall never know, nor if my arrival might have interrupted their extended honeymoon perio in Nigeria. Colony life in West African could be pleasant and enjoyable if your health could stand the climate. Mo insisted, so I am told, that Mabel should join Tony soon after my birth, but not before she and her brother Graham had won the mixed doubles in the Newcastle tennis tournament, a trophy which she had achieved earlier with the Wimbledon player Pat Hughes.

I therefore became part of the household at Ardeevin, spoilt by the cook Nan and a succession of nurses in a family which was expanding at an important time in my grandfather's political life. It is recorded that one of my first words was Boulevard, as I used to be taken in my pram to see the swans on the River Lagan. Other than from photographs, mostly by the sea and probably at Newcastle, I can't recall much of my early childhood except that I remember Sidney's father, Charlie, bringing me my first bicycle, a small green one, and my reaction to the funeral of King George V when I covered my teddy bear in a union jack and put him in a cart as a gun carriage and processed up the street. This must have been after he event, because there was no television to watch and we depended on newspaper photographs .

Do, my grandfather, made a great impression on me at this time; his political life was taking off. He had become a Minister in the Craigavon government, a Privy Councillor after being a back bencher, representing Armagh since the start of the parliament. His business in Portadown was a significant part of his life. I remember him taking me to the Works and seeing a mechanical saw cutting timber, my first experience of industry and I was amazed at the operation. I also recall being with him and Mo on a canvassing occasion; the crowds cheering; the Portadown Feis (a music competition) which was an important event for him. A few years ago I compiled a memoir on him based on the published records of his speeches in the Commons, where he was much revered before having to give up because of illness.

Mo was to be the centre of all our lives for many years. She lived to be a hundred and died in 1970. We all owed her so much and revolved around her pattern of life, ritual and character. She wore blue and pastel colours beautifully chosen and tailored, changing with the season. In the early photographs of the thirties she is in rather drab dress but moved with the times. She had sense of the ridiculous, and would deflate the character of an invited guest before they arrived only to keep us incredulous by treating them then with utmost respect. She suffered from arthritis in one knee which prevented her getting about and in later years this was a great handicap. During the war she did mange trips to London, and they stayed at the Langham Hotel when I met her after a long and tiring journey back to St George's. She entertained lavishly at Melmore and Craigavad, a house to which they moved shortly after Do's illness. As the matriarch she had countless plans for all of us, sporting and otherwise. The feature of the week was the tea on Sunday afternoon, usually after sport at the golf club as church was in the morning. There were a succession of servants but the final one was Margaret Brankin, who became a permanent feature and one of the family, until my aunt Mollie died. The family housed her and we continued to visit her and were always welcome.

Mollie was the daughter who did not marry, as she was of the generation who lost contemporaries in the 1914 war. Tom, the eldest son was killed in the war at Paschendale, which was a great tragedy to the family. Mollie remained at home and, as both her mother and father became infirm, she acted as their secretary and a second parent to the cousins when needed. She came to visit me at school in loco parentis. She was a godmother, confidant and taught me about crosswords, an addiction which she shared with her brother Graham. Suzanne and I have the same addiction today. In the summer of 1948, when I was unwell, I spent some months at Melmore and Auntie Mollie kept me going with chat and talk about what she was doing, her charity work with RUKBA and her golf. When Mo had gone to bed at sharp 10.PM after 9 o'clock tea and watching the boat go down, she would start the crossword and open a tin and say "what about the gorbies"(sweets), a taste which I still have to this day each evening.

By the time I was six there were three cousins ,David, Ken and Joan and I had a sister Paula. The coronation was upon us and Mo and Do went off to Westminster Abbey dressed in the uniform of a Privy Councillor. There is a splendid photo of this. In 1935 we had spent Tony's leave from Nigeria, in Locksbottom, a village outside Bromley where I had got to know the other side of the family, who lived in south London. Tony's father, a doctor, had died when he was thirteen, but there was my widowed grandmother, known as Dabbo, and cousins David and Susan. We also saw the jubilee of George V in whose reign I was born. From their house in Annerley I witnessed the burning of the Crystal Palace with my cousin Susan, who recalls my strong Ulster accent. Her mother Aunt Marjorie was good to me both as visitor to Windsor and the Universal Aunt who saw me from school to holidays and vice versa. Her husband, Freddie, was also in evidence on these occasions and also Brewer, Tony's elder brother, who took me to Lords for the first time in 1944 to a match which was played there before the war ended. He featured in our lives up to the time of his death in 1972. Jane, my other aunt, was a teacher of speech and drama and I was her pupil before my choir trial. I saw one of her productions "Yellow Sands" near Bromley. How interested she would have been in Juliet's theatre career! Sadly she died in 1941 having been bombed out the previous year. Her step children and the next generation have kept in good contact with us as a family. Dabbo died before the war.

8

The Irish great aunts were a regular feature. Auntie Belle (Arabella) and her daughters known as the Dromarts because of their house in Osborne Gardens off the Malone Road was a diminutive woman, dressed in black and white lace, but cheerful. Her sister Gertrude (Callender Bullock) was the flighty one, although she used to send me a bible reading lectionary. Mabel Cather I can barely remember but Marion Shillington Scales lived on the Huntingdon Road in Cambridge, and I used to cycle there for coffee of an evening just for some Irish craik or university gossip. She, and her living-in daughter, Doris, were always glad of news of Belle, the twins Kathleen and Eileen in Belfast, and Edith, an adventurous daughter who went to help in the Sandes homes for soldiers in India.

There was also Doreen Kelly, a relation of the Glenmachan Shillingtons, who lived in considerable wealth in Earlswood Road, Strandtown. She was an inhibited but kind person, who became everyone's godmother or confidant and whose house was always in apple pie order owing to the attentions of her two long term servants, Kitty and Agnes. She surprised everyone by marrying a rich American whom she met while on holiday at Newcastle and her household moved to live on the edge of the Mourne Mountains. Mrs Hamilton, as she became, lived there as a widow and finally looked her two faithful servants as they became elderly. My last recollection was of taking Nicholas to see her. He was able to join her gardener's son fishing at the end of the garden in one of the Mourne streams.

Mabel had been married at Knock Methodist church with a reception at Glenmachan Tower, the home of Do's cousin Courtney Shillington, the Broadway Damask Company. Rives and Maurice, the two sons of Courtney and Bertha, were quite different in character. Rives was in the business , an ADC to the Governor , and he ran the RNVR ship HMS Caroline in Belfast, still to this day the focus of naval training. Maurice became an announcer in the BBC and during the war in London was one of the well known team headed by Stuart Hibbert, who read the news. He returned to Belfast where he continued on radio and eventually television before his retirement. He and his wife Betty were most hospitable whenever we met on either side of the water and he was always good company.

Mabel was named after her aunt, whose son Dermot (the other son Geoffrey was killed at the Somme), married Joyce his cousin and they came to live in Battle. Dermot had been in the Navy. He They were childless and at the end of their lives we inherited a lot of their mementoes, and received legacies.

The other sister Marion, whom I got to know well in my Cambridge days, married a Radiologist Don, Francis Scales, and became Mrs Shillington Scales. Although in her eighties, when I arrived at King's in 1949, she knew Cambridge academic society, being of the generation when dons married and moved out of College and built houses around the backs, where they brought up their families. Her unmarried daughter Doris played the harp and was in demand for Cambridge music, as well as being in the Red Cross which enabled her to be present at university events, congregations, concerts, and anything of interest.

On the Collen side we were taken to se Aunt Bessie (Hamilton Robb) in Deramore Park and Julia the unmarried sister of my grandmother. Visits to great aunts were a feature before returning to boarding school, I presume for inspection and comment on how we were growing up.

My childhood friends were local, but the closest then and for the rest of her life was Sidney Foster. We were born in the same Nursing Home three days apart, she being the elder. Her father was a Civil Servant and her mother the daughter of a well known church of Ireland family. Sidney, a constant participant in this story, started with me at our first school, although I had had some governess teaching with my friend John Pim, son of Sir Richard who went on the Churchill's staff in the war.

After living on our own in Cherry Valley Gardens, and then in Green Road Knock where Miles was born, our household was augmented by the arrival of Ella Atchison, an auburn haired girl in her teens from the Scottish borders, and who was to be our nurse until the outbreak of war. As she had a camera, this was a source of our childhood memories, and she even went as far as to enter a photograph of my sister Paula for a baby competition which she won, although she had not asked Mabel's permission to do so. She was recruited by Jack Shillington, Mabel's elder brother, who also found nurses for his family and my other cousins the Wheelers. We all congregated at Newcastle, Co Down for holidays, in a house on the hill where there on which I loved to play. That was 1937 and there is a group photo of Miles' christening and they are all obviously enjoying life. Another year I remember being at Miss Norman's boarding house, where a fisherman used to arrive with lobsters, landed at the harbour and brought strapped to his bicycle. He used to race them cross the kitchen floor. I spent much time below stairs as a child which I enjoyed.

Mo and Do moved from Ardeevin to Melmore in Craigavad a place which was to become the focus of the family from then until Uncle Graham died in 2001. The nursing of Do took up much of their time but they used to drop in at Helen's Bay, and I well remember Do being with us in September 1939 when we heard the broadcast of Neville Chamberlain saying that we were at war.

It must have been after 1937 that Mabel rented a house called Sheridan Lodge in Helen's Bay on the shores of Belfast Lough. There was the beach and a village school run as a dame school by Miss Jefferson, a stately lady who seemed able to control a room full of different age groups all pursuing individual stages of learning. Eventually she had to cope with both James Douglas and Miles in the same class! Having moved from Strandtown, Belfast, from a large primary school to a village school, there were fewer children my own age. I became friendly with Alan Cook, who was the same age and we remain friends to this day. I was best man at his wedding in London. There were also the Greeves family in nearby Crawfordsburn, Tony, Mary and Kerry Greeves ,who was at Cambridge when I was . The ambience of Helens Bay included a wood known as the Drive where it was good to play. It was a place for children and their imagination to take off, with wooded walks along the beach which you could walk all the way to Bangor some six miles away. Whitewashed Irish cottages at the end of lanes and the views of the coastline made County Down special. It was so easy to cycle in those days, across Craigantlet or to the Ards, without helmets helped, if lucky, by a three speed gear, but nothing more sophisticated. Along the shore there was the boat house where Mr Gilmour, a retired bank manager, kept a boat, much to the envy of us all. His daughter ran the dancing class where the girls went. Into this came Hilda Douglas with her three children Ann, James and Mary, who all moved in with us at Sheridan Lodge. Mary still lives in Helen's Bay there and is a constant source of memories about this village, which was in some ways a typical "British" community, with church, sport and shopping linking it. There were a number of English families living there who commuted to Stormont by train.

The war brought us more together and we had Air raid wardens, Home Guard and various unit of the armed forces based at Grey Point, a sort of army barracks located on the shore to keep out hostile shipping. It was during this time that Barry Widnell, Jane's stepson, came to stay on local leave before being sent to Sicily where he was killed on active service in the Honorable Artillery Company.

Do died in January 1944 and then during the summer holidays we received a Sunday morning visit from the postmistress with a telegram to say that Jimmy Douglas had been killed in Normandy. Mabel took charge instantly and I was deputed to take all the children to the beach, while Hilda prepared herself for telling the children. Tony arrived for leave at unexpected moments due to convoy movements from West Africa; once he arrived unannounced and Paula was shocked to see her mother kissing a "strange man" at the gate, much to his chagrin. People have said that Ulster didn't experience the effects of the war but for us the war effort went on. We had troops stationed there, and an anti aircraft battery on the golf course. Both Kitty Stephens and Maureen Gabby had husbands who were serving, so it was not all that unlike the films which we saw about other villages in Britain during wartime. I remember being quite frightened during the air raids on Belfast in 1941. They seemed so near.

Family life flourished after the war; the younger ones put on plays for the family entertainment, and I had my first experience of organising cricket at Melmore during the summer and teaching the younger ones the rudiments of the game. By this time Jack Shillington, who commanded his regiment and had won the DSO in Normandy, had been wounded and invalided out of the army and came to live in Ulster and played with us. Mollie Wheeler was deputed to be his runner. The Douglas family must have joined us for this in 1946, as the photos show, and so began a relationship on the cricket field with James, who now joins us at Cowden each summer to play on the village ground.

Another feature of Helens Bay was the orchestra which met at Sheridan lodge. We recruited Tony Greeves and other violinists, Clare Johnston and June Shuttleworth; Mabel played the cello and I the clarinet in favourites such as Lilac Time, Greensleeves and of course the Londonderrry Air, which remains in the family repertoire. Music around the piano or the action songs at Christmas were a feature of Melmore, where my Tony or Jack's wife Holly played the piano. She once taught me how to play three in one hand against two in the other. Both Tony and Mabel got much from Helens Bay. He had more time there after the war ended and flights made it easier to travel to Nigeria for shorter tours of duty. He enjoyed church life there and got involved with arranging music for services. Mabel did the salvage during the war and worked in the forces canteen when she met Hilda

11

Douglas. I remember the awful Camp coffee that they used to serve to the troops. Surprisingly Tony made friends with Hugh Moore a businessman and farmer with extreme Protestant views, but he was around at the time of a tragic accident to their son, who lost a leg.   Hugh and Mollie Moore became lifelong friends of the family. Paula got much from the brownies and mixing with other girls of her own age. Brownies of course were a feature of her later life. By a coincidence the widow of a vicar of Helens Bay turned up to live near them in Cheltenham. At Helen's Bay Miles got his love for the sea and used to spend time looking for goodies among the flotsam. This was a special for us.

At this time too Mo was able to see her sons succeed in their careers as Jack came to run the Territorial Army office in Northern Ireland and Graham came back from duty in Derry in 1956 to become Commissioner of the Royal Ulster Constabulary (RUC) in Belfast. Graham now had three children, Colin, Anthony and Eve. On the distaff side both Jim and Tony were making their way. Family parties, wedding anniversaries, and social life at the golf club for bridge, and entertaining (the days of temperance seemed to fade) became a part of Mo's widowhood. Glencraig Church and regular visits to the business in Portadown, which continued to flourish, made for happier post war years for the family, those who worked for them and the growing circle of friends. So as not to move, Mo built a bungalow in the garden, a single story version of the important rooms of Melmore in which she, Mollie and then Graham lived there until 2001. It was for us permanence in changing world. I brought my own children when they were small to see their great grandmother in the 1960s, and she sang them the same lullabies as she did to me and continued to take a great interest in them.

For me it was a happy time and my diaries which merely record incident and activity show that I fitted in to both school and home without being affected by the difference. I did spend some time at local prep school, Rockport during the excesses of the blitz. Before war started Mabel had taken me to the launching of HMS Belfast in 1938. This ship is now based in London. She also ensured that I got to the theatre in Belfast, the Ulster Group Theatre which ran a series of repertory plays, but had to compete with the boxing going on in the adjacent Ulster Hall. The standard of acting was as good as I was to find in the famous Windsor repertory where were allowed to go as a treat at St George's.

After Helen's Bay, Paula, Miles and I spent more of the holidays at Melmore, where it was good to be together with our cousins, but Helen's Bay had been our first family home. My friend, Alan Cook, of whom I saw a lot of then and who I met again in 2009, share memories of growing up in that community during war, the air raids, the beaching of the Sunderland flying boat and the celebration of Victory in Japan day in August 1945 when we made a huge bonfire. I was later to spend a summer at Melmore when I was recovering from my tubercular gland in 1948 and sadly missed an important summer term. However Alan and I together with Sidney Foster and her girl friends had a summer of tennis parties during the summer of 1947, a landmark in our lives.

I came to value the circle of cousins, eventually twelve, as I grew older, and to be able to share as adults the background and reminiscences of youth and of growing up in the environment which Mo, who lived to be a hundred, created around her. Friendship with cousins deepened as and when the business of bringing up children had concluded and we began to enjoy each other's company and a common sense of humour. This may have been because we got to know more about genes and likenesses developed as grew older. The wedding of Eve to Alan Parkhill brought us together. I was close to my uncle and godfather Graham and visited him regularly at Ardeevin which he took over from Mo.

The Shillington family history is yet to be completed by my cousin Anthony who has already researched the early years and continues to trace and find new links, working with the Craigavon Historical Society. His efforts will I am sure complete this record for what has become a very large connection, to use the Irish expression. My cousin Susan is tracing the Shillingfords, their origins in Exeter and Buckinghamshire. There was once a drapers shop in Greenwich. The medical connection goes back some way before our grandfather, Frank Norton, Dabbo' husband, practiced in south London. On both sides of the family we exchange memories, photos and gossip when we meet, if only for social occasions such as Glyndebourne. It is indicative of a happy and interested upbringing as letters, the main means of communication at that time, show how we were fortunate to be given such a good start to our lives.

Jack Shillington died in 1972 and after that his wife Aunt Holly continued to live in Melmore until her death when it was sold. Mollie died in 1977 at eighty but Peggy, Graham's wife, had died earlier that year, a great gap in all our lives. The Wheeler family had moved from Belfast to Craigavad and Beth continued to live there until 1985 so the continuity of the area was very evident. Of my cousins, Ken Wheeler remained in Ulster as did Colin, David and Eve Shillington, the rest moving away.

It was the unexpected discovery in the 1990s of Patricia Collen, daughter of Mo's brother Ritchie that brought the family more together. She had spent seventy one years as an inpatient at Normansfield Hospital in Teddington, a hospital founded by Langford Down for learning disabled. As described by Andy Merriman in his book Tales of Normansfield the Langdon Down Legacy "during all these epoch making events (1926-1997) Patricia because of her physical disabilities and a mild mental handicap of an unknown origin had spent most of her life institutionalised" Shortly before the hospital closed, and Patricia was settled in the community, the Court of Protection searched for any relative. Miles, because of his Chancery links, was involved and put me forward as a named relative. I became a trustee of her Settlement Trust and, ultimately, her Receiver and then Deputy. I was able to understand the need to find a suitable lifestyle for her. As a non-executive director of a health trust, I was already experienced in resettlement of sufferers from learning disabilities and their placements in residential accommodation in the community. With the Official Solicitor we purchased a house from Patricia's estate and arranged for it to be shared with others. Eventually, it seemed more sensible for her to have it as her own house with dedicated and living in carers. These changes greatly improved the setting as it became more home like and the family gradually learned to know how to interact with her. As quoted in the book, at the time when Michelle and George Whitmore, her final carers were looking after her "the extent of her activities has now been tailored to suit her needs and enthusiasms and she has become the centre of attention. Compared to the shy lady of Normansfield, she is now much more open and communicative and is now able to share laughter and music with children and adults in the neighbourhood".

physical disabiliteisare now given In 2007 she visited Portadown, the home of both the Shillingtons and the Collens. She also went to a garden Party at Buckhingham Palace I Want to go out" was a favourite expression and she did go out every day either for lunch in a restaurant, Hampton Court, Richmond Park and theatre. Known locally as the "little Lady of Teddington", her lifestyle during the final fifteen years of her life were the best which she had ever had.

As Merriman says "Who knows what she may have achieved in her lifetime, given the opportunities that some children with learning and? Despite the fact that Patricia's family were extremely well heeled, she was denied the possibility of a life fulfilled"

The Collen great grandparent's portraits hang in our house,in Gigouzac in France as a reminder of this heritage. Patricia's birthday parties, an idea from Paddy Shillington, became a regular occasion in February for the cousins to meet and even sing with her. After her death in 2010 part of he estate was given to charities working with people of all ages, including help to families with young children, who have similar problems which she had.

CHAPTER 3

Faire is the Heaven

Russell Thorndike, author and actor describes the choristers of St Georges Chapel Windsor as "Children of the Garter;" a special phrase and one to be revered. He was writing in the last years of Victoria's reign, when the Yorkshire man Walter Parratt was organist and Master of the Choristers. I had read his book or rather Mabel read it to me so I was familiar with the saga and mystique that attached to St Georges and Travers College, now the school, but once the home of the naval knights, as distinct from the military nights who ran amok in drunkenness and were expelled. Being educated in grounds owned by the Crown was a privilege. In our day we played our games in the Home Park, across the Datchet Road, whereas nowadays the greatly enlarged school have access to the private park through the gate in the wall. We did get to walk in that park where it was said that Queen Victoria used to walk and the gardeners had to hide in caves so that they would not be seen.

I arrived as a chorister in September 1939 just after war had broken out. I didn't react badly to boarding and it didn't seem to make much difference. My diary briefly says that I went to England. Mabel left me at school and so began my time as a boarder aged 8. I was surrounded by other choristers - Daman, Price, Bell, Harland and Kidner, unfamiliar names for me but there was one called McClure. There were sons of famous musicians such as Sargent, Sumsion and Statham. My fellow new boys were Pasteur and Peter Sumsion. I can't recall how long it was before I was robed and singing in chapel, but I was up for anything. I got a part in the school play, but at that stage wasn't one of those who stayed for Christmas. In the summer term there was an epidemic of chicken pox and German measles. Sufferers had to be isolated in the chapter garden, where I recall reading about the Graf Spee.

I think that I was on Cantoris to begin with and got to enjoy the music of Stanford and Wesley in particular and I picked up the repertoire quickly and without difficulty. I somehow learnt to sight read although I was always inclined to trust my ear ahead of my eyes. Daily psalm singing, antiphonally, was a routine which I began to appreciate and I soon came to memorise and say the words, a facility which has remained with me throughout my life. I still read my Psalter during the week. I was fascinated by heraldry and the banners of the knights of the Garter which hung over the stalls at Windsor. I used to fix my eyes on them during service, and got to know the names of the families represented there. I felt an affinity with the banner of the Marquess of Londonderry, whose home at Mount Stewart was not far from us in County Down. Another Irish garter knight was the Duke of Abercorn We were all in chapel when the banner of the Emperor of Japan was removed and we ceremoniously stamped on it to state our disgust.

We sang 12 services a week and had practices on most days except Wednesday. We had to sing unaccompanied services on Fridays when we tried out much of the

Tudor music by Byrd and others which was coming off the press, edited by Edmund Horace Fellows, a minor canon of a stern and solemn countenance, who was the nearest to an ascetic that I have met. The Matron, appropriately called Miss Leach, watched over our health and made sure that we were not overworked or run down by this schedule. Stiff Eton collars were confined to chapel use except on Sundays when we wore the short Eton jacket. My mother recalls taking me and a friend out for exeat and hiring a carriage. We both sat with the driver like something from a Charles Dickens television costume drama.

Much of the pageantry of the Order of the garter was suspended during the war but we did have the military knights in residence. When Evens the senior verger used to proclaim Tolls Down, indicating the start of the service, the knights used to clank their spurs as they processed into the choir in front of us.

The chapel was run by Dean Albert Baillie, a godson of Queen Victoria, (his mother had been a lady in waiting), and three canons, Anthony Deane, who wrote for Punch, Stafford Crawley, an ex padre, and Sidney Ollard, an historian of the Oxford movement. The centre of our lives was William Henry Harris, or Doc H as we called him, who rehearsed us daily and of whom we became fond, despite his bates when we had sung badly, when his lower lip protruded. He was a benign professorial type, a cross between Dr Doolittle and a older version of Harry Potter, married to deaf but kind Doris with two welcoming daughters, Margaret and Ann known as Squibs, who, despite war service, seemed to be a large part of our lives. Tea with them and the Crawleys was a treat on Sundays despite rationing.

Doc Hs was a very modest musician, a great performer and teacher at the College of Organists, and a composer, companion and friend of many of his contemporaries such a Vaughan Williams, Walford Davies, E.J. Morean, and George Dyson. He hated conducting in the chancel, which he had to do on Fridays when services were unaccompanied and he couldn't hide in the organ loft and glare at us. On these occasions he sat with us in the stalls and gave us the note on the pitch pipe. Fridays were therefore a day for Tudor music and because the Rev Dr Edmund Horace Fellowes, editor of Byrd, Tallis and Morley, was a resident minor canon, many new editions kept coming our way. However we did sing some Palestrina and other Italian music.

Harris is remembered today for the double choir motet which is my title, "Faire is the Heaven," written in D Flat, his favourite key and a fitting memorial to his love of twentieth century polyphony and the cathedral accoustic. I can sense his smile each time I hear 'Archangels, archangels...' before it side steps into that beautiful passage as its ending "the image of such endless perfectness." The words are from hymn o f heavenly beautie by Edmund Spenser. His idea of heaven certainly rubbed off on me. I have a treasured pocket score of Brahms 3rd Symphony inscribed by him as my leaving present, when he had tagged on to the fact that I was beginning to like recordings of orchestras and enjoyed following them with a score. John Forster came as assistant organist when Alwyn Surplice was called up. He was a gentle man, who became a great friend until the end of his life. He was so patient with me, and found time to understand my potential in music. War did not deprive us of good teachers.

Besides music, there was the academic side of school, sport and the plays. After a time James Webb Jones, headmaster, and Jock Burnett went to war service. The new headmaster was Philip Cavenaugh , an older man, whose family took over and his daughter Betty, a pretty woman was one of the first of our woman teachers . Of the masters, Aubrey Havard was to feature in my life regularly until his death at Charterhouse where I used to visit him in the 1980s. I was not one of his scholarship boys, but I did make his unbeaten 1942 soccer team.   The team photograph remained on the wall of his room. John Forster took me in hand and enabled me to get a music scholarship. He took me the National Gallery concerts organised by Myra Hess. He also composed a song for me to sing in the school play. We kept in contact and he and Mollie visited us shortly before his death. The St Georges musical plays were by a former master Mr Bridg; period dramas with puns a la W.S.Gilbert, which provided suitable moments for song either ensemble or solo. For years generations of old boys would return to the school for the plays and sit and sing the encores at the back of the theatre.

All this went on while doodle bugs were falling, fathers, brothers and masters were being killed in action, including a boy called Falwasser, whose sister I was to meet on the shores of Loch Etive some forty years later . Among my younger contemporaries were other famous musical families, Jacques, Havergal, Newell, Nightingale and the effervescent James Owen, who later became a canon, who could be relied upon to reduce us to stitches in chapel by imitating the faces of the regulars in the congregation.

The time when my voice was at its best was summer 1943 when I was solo boy. I managed to sing several of the solo anthems, and the Messiah recitatives at Christmas. In 1944 I became head chorister, and took part in the only ceremonial service of my time, the installation of Dean Eric Hamilton. I enjoyed cricket, and won the fielding cup and the Nelson prize for contribution to school life. I finished in the Christmas term of 1944 with the funeral of Queen Victoria's youngest daughter, Princess Beatrice, several royal christenings and the confirmation of the future QueenElizabeth II. I had won my music scholarship to Trent.

I cannot fail to mention the contact we had with the domestic life of the royal family, which is where this memoir started on the steps of the royal apartments in the Castle. Because it was war time, the Queen and her daughters spent much time at Windsor, and it must have been home to them. Education was part of the regimen for the princesses and Henry Marten, the history teacher at Eton could be spotted arriving in his coach for their history lessons. They also were taught with families on the estate and it was with these children that they performed pantomimes at Christmas. The Waterloo chamber was transformed into pantomime world, the frames which normally held the kings of England being replaced King Cole, Jack and the beanstalk, Aladdin and goodness knows who. (I am told by the guides that they are still there today below the restored majesties which are displayed to visiting heads of states.) Music had to be part of the education and that was where Doc H and the choristers came in. He gave them piano lessons, but the experience of singing in a choir was as important as being in a pantomime. Four of us were allowed to escape chapel duties and to join a hand-picked choir of SATB voices (not the lay clerks) drawn from Windsor and Eton Choral Society, the College, the regiments and wherever. Crawfie, their governess, was also part of this choir. We sat with the royal princesses in the red drawing room facing the west terrace, and sang Gibbons "The silver Swan," "Fine Knacks for ladies," "Grensleeves" and a number of other songs from the Oxford Song Book, which Doc H had selected. Sometimes we shared our copies, sometimes we sat between the girls. The recollections for us are a legion. It was a relaxed and friendly occasion, Doc H fussing in his nervous and caring way. At the end of term we were invited to tea and to perform before the Queen, but much to Doc H' s displeasure we sang sharp. No chance of the usual telling off or bate, he bowed sweetly and said "Sheer excitement Ma'am" and we all stopped for tea. We were also invited to the Waterloo Chamber to see the pantomime "Puss in Red Riding Boots" written and produced by Mr Tanner from the estate and in which the two girls sang "Swinging on a star " a topical Bing Crosby number, the future queen making a delightful principal boy. She was an inspiration to all the young, and to whom at that time, I took quite a fancy, whether in uniform or taking part in the war effort.

It could be regarded these days, as a deprivation to spend our Christmas, Easter and early August at school where we were required for chapel services. There were, however, various entertainments, such as the Dean's party and a game of murder in the Deanery, a theatre trip to the well known Windsor Repertory Company, and the royal family came to services as they still do to this day. There was always plenty of excitement and people to share it with. The masters made our lives interesting and we became our own personalities early in life.

I still have a personal Christmas card drawn and written by Aubrey Havard, and I assume he did this for all of us.

Dear Shillers of Sheridan Lodge
Though at your meals you don't stodge
You have manners polite
But I do think you might
Your dear Mr Gecks sometimes dodge.

Mr Gecks was my clarinet teacher at Eton and I sometimes missed Mr Havard's lessons for my clarinet lesson.

Over the years I have returned to Windsor for services in chapel and for reunions. As a young man I would play in the cricket match, but it would always be followed by chapel, and latterly the service would be a dedicated one to the school, with familiar music by Walter Parratt and Parry's "Jerusalem" which we all sang in the commemoration of benefactors known as the obit service. Kings have a similar service on Founders day. In 2008 we went to an evensong to commemorate the life of Robert Ward, a chorister who had committed much of his life and spare time to the keeping together of the "Old Boys" as we were at first called. It struck me then that whenever we go back to service in chapel there is a bonding between all of us who have ever stood in those choir stalls. We_automatically become part of the service, recognising and anticipating every note. What amazed me then was to see older men like John Denison, a Parratt chorister, whom I used to meet at cocktail parties. I now realise that Patrick Harland and I who, usually go together, must now appear like that to those much younger as we all retrace our lives as choristers, inwardly singing along in the psalms or responses. Perhaps that which draws us together is the memory of Doc H, his moods and his fame for "Faire is the Heaven" now sung in so many places and ecordings. It is an anthem that, in our tim, this shy man would neglect to perform because of criticism and bullying from his traditional and died- in- the- wool lay clerks, such as Kempton and Simpkins. What a breed they were, but a part of us, and I still get that special feeling when the train pulls out of the station and Windsor castle disappears, or when it comes into sight and I walk from the station and hear the sound of children playing at the school playground, alongside the Royal Oak pub. I well remember kicking the ball over so that we could nip in and see if any masters were there. So many ghosts, happy ones crowd into my memory.

CHAPTER 4

"The grassy plains of Derby"
from the School song by J.H.Gower

"On the grassy plains of Derby,
In the heart of England old,
Where a river murmurs to its banks
A tale that's never told.
There lives a band of comrades true,
A band that's ne'er been rent,
Since the river to the College gave,
The glorious name of Trent."

It was January 1945 and not the best time to be exchanging the splendour of Windsor for industrial Long Eaton in the Midlands. I recall the glow from the Stanton Ironworks visible from the dormitory window. I was in Wright House,and although Trent was small school at that time of some 160 boys for me it sedmed quite large. I had been warned of initiation into the Junior Common Room, and that one had to show ones manliness by telling a joke, so I was prepared and as a musical boy among a number of philistines, to a degree, I had to find my metier.

As in all first years at a new school it was a time for acclimatisation and 1945 was a year which saw the end of the War. In May we had a holiday for Victory in Europe followed by a general election. It was also my first experience of Nottingham, which became twenty years later the place where I worked, and a community which I got to know well through being President of the Junior Chamber of Commerce, and in which Edward, Marianne and my grandchildren still live.

I recall both music and drama. As it was the end of war, we sang as a chamber choir a setting of Rupert Brooke's "If I should die" by Alan Gray at Comem, our annual summer speech day. There was another ex chorister Ronald Arnatt from King's.   I was cast as Helena in the school play Midsummer Night's Dream. However to the dismay of Bill Melton the drama directo,r my voice started to break and I put on a stone in weight so the painted maypole became something of a bag! However he was not put off by this, and I was allowed to polish my dramatic talents in roles such as the Archbishop in St Joan, Claudius in Hamlet. I developed a stage presence for bland sanctimonious speeches, which I still have, and finally Poskett in Pinero's The Magistrate. Bill Melton was a great actor and teacher. He would stop the clock of syllabus and bring something of poetry and drama into our lives. It was his sense of fun and lack of seriousness which appealed. He once said that he and I would do Mrs Malaprop and Sir Lucius O'Trigger as a school play, quite monstrous really for a master to appear in drag! It was sad that our paths never crossed at Glyndebourne where he was an extra for many years and where I became an usher and met some of those with whom he had been on stage.

As a small school I was up for everything and enjoyed sport, and swimming in a newly built and heated pool named after the head Ford Ikin. The Corps was commanded by my housemaster Charles Lang supported by Sergeant Major Kemp, who arrived in my time and ended as a Trent legend. He also played the timpani in the school orchestra. We all paraded twice a week, did shooting and learnt about weapons, and took tests. I appear in uniform in the school history being inspected by the Duke of Devonshire. I rose to the rank of sergeant and went to camp at Catterick   In the history sixth, I came under John Loder, an elegantly dressed west country man, racing correspondent for the Field, who wrote elegant prose He taught us that we should read the middle page of the Times each day, particularly the fourth leader and the correspondence. Loder was critical of my foray into the arts which were for him and what he called "greenery yallery," a Gilbertian phrase. He summed me up well in my final report "need to guard against a possible tendency to be too easily satisfied with his achievements, mistaking exceptional competence for remarkable distinction." A lesson I should have learnt as it is a fault of mine to this day.

Like most single sex public schools at this time, the pupils were sons of professional and middle class parents, and one never met anyone from a different ethnic background. Trent had a pre war tradition of accepting pupils from Siam. In fact one of these became prime minister and in my time paid a visit to the school and gave a talk. He was an amusing and intelligent man well versed in the social arts. Towards the end of my time a Siamese boy came to the school, an indication of the return of normal international relations after the war.

Most of the boys came from the north of England or the midlands, and I came to recognise their accents. The use of the word one (pronounced wan) was distinctive. We had boys from Yorkshire, Lancashire and even a as far as Cumbria. My ear had been used to Ulster and southern England accents so it was a change, which stood me in good stead when I came back to Nottingham and Mansfield later in life.

We came by train and on arrival at Trent junction, which was on the main Midland line, there was a sign 'for Trent College', and from there it was a taxi ride to College. Our luggage trunk had been sent PLA in advance , with a tuck box, and we only had our overnight case for the first few days. Our tuck box, a small hinged container about 3 feet by eighteen inches, had our goodies, food and special objects which went into the common room and was locked. Eventually, as prefects we were entitled to studies, either with another or on our own, and we spread our where withal widely and even had others in for tea or coffee between work and duties. It felt very grown up and we enjoyed the company of our peers. In my case it happened when I was quite young, and I , and I learnt to hold my own with older and more mature boys at a time when age made a great difference between us.

Freedom was given according to age and status. There were no games on Sunday, the evangelical tradition of Trent prevailing. We were however allowed to buy our own Sunday newspaper, one of which serialised the book "Forever Amber"! Walks to Sawley Oak and Draycott were the order of the day and we were allowed to cycle in the summer term. I well remember the long summer Saturday evenings and playing grass court tennis on the court outside the headmaster's house until the shadows lengthened and lights out was announced by one of our trumpeters playing the last post on the terrace. Boarding had its delights, particularly for me, as I was a long way from home and visits for leave outs few. We wore dark suits on Sunday, and had two chapel services, with sermons and Holy Communion for the confirmed. Each day we had a service in chapel with hymns. Our daily uniform was a brown tweed jacket, grey flannel trousers, collar and tie, and black shoes. When emancipated we blossomed into colour to flaunt the sombre convention.

Mornings were different, as it was a before the days of showers, and we started the day by leaping into a cold bath, filled the night before and there could be a coating of ice if it was winter and freezing outside. The school rule said "Every boy must have a cold bath every morning on rising unless he has "leave off" from either the school doctor or his Housemaster." This was a left over from an early headmaster's rule, the Rev J.S.Tucker Trent had been founded by evangelicals in response to the Woodard schools, whom we played against in matches, going as far as Ellesmere in Lancashire. The foundation stone had been laid by the Duke of Devonshire, the Derbyshire grandee from Chatsworth and the family connection with the school is retained to this day.

Tucker came back to preach in July 1947. Taking as his text the school motto *Sapientia est fons vitae,* he traced the sequence of quotations on wisdom from scripture for spiritual growth, and then went on to talk about mental growth. Books such as Lord Jim, Westward Hoe and the biography of Robert Louis Stevenson were essential to develop the mind and to make us into good citizens living a life to which God had called us. A classic sermon of its time, and a theme which at that time Trent was keen to pursue in both sermon and song at Commemoration. Eric Thiman's "Songs of England" and Quilters "Non nobis Domine" being musical examples.

I got to know the city of Nottingham well through trips in Barton buses. Being devoid of parental visits, I made my own excursions to the city on leave out days, when I went to its cinemas and often Charles Lang would commission me to change his library book at Boots in Pelham Street.

During the winter of 1947 things were at a standstill as far as organised games went. There was a continuous freeze until March. We played ice hockey on the open air old swimming pool, which was never covered, and one day a few of us skated along the canal from long Eaton to Derby, passing close by Draycott where Marianne's parents now have their house.

The other institution at Trent was the Rev G J S Warner, either called Daddy or Plug. He was a pipe smoking cleric of the broad church to which I was used. In addition to chapel, where I became a warden and attended him at Holy Communion 8 am, he was ahead of his time on environment and recycling. His passion was the grounds of Trent and he had devised a system of trees, spinneys planted by visiting bishops and politicians, and named and catalogued for all to learn. His organisation of "navvies" helped to recycle and turn over compost in a way which would have gladdened the hearts of the organic fraternity of the twenty first century. "Navvying", as the school rules said, was an alternative form of the compulsory exercise which we had to take each day. It was sad that I only became interested in this side of things as an adult after he had shuffled off this mortal coil, but I am eternally grateful to him for inculcating something in me which stood the test of time.

Ford Ikin and Charles Lang were other mentors. Ikin was hard to get to know but he knew how to train his pupils and together with Betty his wife, they taught us social graces through invitations to dinner at his home. The toughest of these was when he invited the pianist Kathleen Long to play a recital to us. I, aged 17, was to make the vote of thanks at the concert which took place on 22nd November 1947, so I was invited to dinner. I had worked up all sorts of conversational topics on the analysis of Beethoven sonatas, only to be tongue tied when she and Betty spent the meal discussing recipes. It was an early lesson that music and food went well together. Ikin also taught me how to read the lesson in chapel, and I was privileged to be asked to accompany him to chapel, when he wanted to rehearse his reading and projection of the famous Binyon lines for commemoration.

I owe him my place at King's. As a King's choral scholar himself, he would have liked me to follow him but that was not to be. However through him I was invited for interview in March 1948 and met Patrick Wilkinson the Tutor and of course Donald Beves, who organised a trip to the Arts to see "Troilus and Cressida". A letter from Patrick suggests that I might have been better suited to try the English scholarship at King's, but somehow with two parents who had read history, and a possible future in administration, history was my chosen subject. My diaries at Trent indicate that I was interested in journalism, and I remember writing an essay on T.S Eliot which was read to the form, so Patrick might have been right.

Charles Lang, my housemaster in Wright, named after our founder, treated me as an adult. When I became head of his house we would sit in his sparsely furnished room, while he had his gin and we would discuss the joint management of our people and resources. A good lesson in management of people. He corresponded with me when I was ill to keep me in touch, and he was responsible for my first visit to Trent Bridge. Of course when I came back after I left I was able to sit with him and drink gin. When I left he wrote a nice report saying "a useful and effective head of house and has done it without the help of prestige in games, which makes it all the more creditable." In fact it was his confidence in me which really counted.

Trent was a school of some 160 boarders with no day boys. We were divided into four houses but during my time an additional house was added and the old sanatorium developed. There was heart-searching when we knew that present arrangements would be broken up to make up the new house and the set up which we had known since arrival would be disturbed. The new housemaster was to be Godfrey Harland, the elder brother of my friend Patrick from St George's, who must have had difficult task as a new arrival, but he seemed to enter well into things and we became close through music, as he was a horn player in the school orchestra, and later we were to meet him when he took on the military school at Welbeck Abbey.

My progress in the school was as expected. As a music scholar, I played and sang as required although my relations with the director of music were not good. Maybe it was because I tried to enter into everything that was going, such a drama and sport, but I made my way academically and took my set exams as planned until I had to drop out in the summer of 1948 because of TB gland trouble. Because of this I missed out on being head of School and probably my rugby colours but if all had gone as planned, I could have become arrogant and insufferable and might never have arrived at King's.

A highlight of the music for me was the chance to play in the Mozart wood wind quintet at the summer concert in 1946 when I was fifteen. By all accounts it was a good performance and I have the programme signed by all of us. There just happened to be four of us at the standard to play this work at the school concert, one of whom was John Birch who became organist and choirmaster of Chichester Cathedral and whom I continued to meet from time to time. The piece has so much of Mozart in it that I yearn to go back to it. Birch also played Mozart Piano Concerto No 24 in C minor (K491), with the orchestra, of which I was a member, before he left for the Royal College of Music. I was lucky to be at Trent at this time with such good musicians as companions.

Trent broadened my outlook and I learnt much from my teachers. Ikin taught me to read in chapel where he used to rehearse me in particular the first chapter of St John. Melton was poetry and drama and instilled in me a love of opera; from Loder I learnt succinct essay writing and reading the Times; from Lang conversation and management of people.

I made a number of friends. Alan Mould who also went to Cambridge and became headmaster of St John's School when my sons were there, John Herklots who also arrived at Cambridge after me and became ordained, and Robin Perry a resident and lover of the Lake District, whose parents were very kind to me, as I was often without family on leave out days. During my last year we had an intake of boys in Wright one of whom was Neil Howlett, with whom I kept up during his career as an opera singer, and David (Lord) Gilmore who rose to be head of the Foreign Service.

I left for Kings in 1949 and on arrival there found older Old Tridents well ensconced on one staircase, most of whom had done war service, and were mature men compared with me, a schoolboy. I was accepted into the club and returned to Trent with one who was a lawyer, to debate against the school. Ford Ikin came to Kings often and he and his wife Betty appeared at a May Ball at Kings when I danced with her .My remaining contact at a much later stage was with Tim Bowles, a close friend, who despite his ill feeling over the disposal of Bramcote, where he was headmaster, Ikin's worst decision, became a governor and champion of the school until his death in 2005.

CHAPTER 5

The way we lived then

So what was the world like when I was twenty in 1950? Our bedrooms were cold when we got up in the morning and we wore flannel pyjamas and heavy serge dressing gowns. Without central heating, we shivered as we dressed. At Kings there was no en suite and we tottered across the courtyard in the open air to the bathroom in our dressing gowns. For breakfast, served cafeteria style, food was still rationed, so we each brought our tray of butter, sugar and marmalade. Eggs were rationed but I had been allowed extra dairy foods because of my illness. Bread, white or brown, loaves unsliced, were staple diet, and at the shop they cost 4 pence and one farthing. A farthing was a quarter of an old penny. Petrol was in short supply except for essential users such a doctors, but Mo had a car and used to go shopping in Belfast. She had two servants, a cook and a house parlour maid. People still had nurses, although Ella had left at the beginning of war, when Mabel, no longer going to Nigeria, decided to look after us and learn how to cook. She had an old car which was not really practical. After the war they got a car while on leave from Nigeria, so we had the use of it at home. Few undergraduates had cars or were allowed to keep them, although dare devils flaunted this rule. We cycled everywhere even to the playing field at Barton Road and back after games for baths in College. Cycles had to be numbered in Cambridge but we cycled without helmets, quite safely without any fear of accident or need of special lanes.

My visits to England both before and when I went to school were by boat in a cabin overnight, then a train at dawn either from Heysham or Liverpool. The train journey usually took most of the day arriving at Euston in late afternoon. I might spend a night with Auntie Marjorie or go straight to St George's. Coming back i arrived in Belfast in time for breakfast, a real treat after term time shortages. There was a special time when Uncle Brewer took me to Lords on the way home in 1943 , after cricket started up again. At Trent when I had my own study as a prefect, we were allowed to make toast, tea and other goodies bought from the tuck shop or pantry, but under strict rules of safety.

Refrigerators were rare, and food was kept in a larder, a room off the kitchen with stone shelves, a small window, usually wire netted to keep out flies, and various vessels to preserve food like eggs, meat and vegetables. Eggs were preserved in crocks filled with a liquid called isinglass and meat was kept in a covered muslin cage. The cooker could be a range, a black solid fuel (coal) cooker and water heater, with ovens, hob for boiling kettles and an open fire for toasting bread. In the days before supermarkets, shopping was done frequently, locally and items were not stored for long periods. Grocers, in brown coats, called to take the order and it was delivered to the house later. Vegetables were only available according to season, which could be boring, or available in tins. There were also tine of pilchards, sardines and jam which came from countries of the commonwealth such as Australia or South Africa. If eggs were not available we had dried egg powder. Ice creams were bought from shops or vans – 'stop me and buy one' was emblazoned on the side, either as cones or sliders (two wafers with a block between), and were not desserts. Fish was in good supply from fishmongers, particularly if you lived near the coast. There were three sorts of shops for food, grocers, green grocers, for vegetables and fishmongers.

Telephone calls were made through an operator at a local exchange, and we had to identify the town or district by name and then the number. One always thought that they might be listening in if you were having an intimate chat. Hence we didn't telephone much. Today one can elucidate the London district by the alphabetical place of the numbers in the exchange code i.e. 228 Battersea. In fact when I first started work, all calls were connected through an operator. While she was dialling, there was the chance of a chat with the telephonist. Secretaries fielded calls as appropriate, but we never had the facility for direct dialling until about the eighties.

Television? One was in the common room at King's and I remember seeing the varsity match when I came up for my exam in 1948. Most houses just had a radio called a wireless. In the thirties these were run off batteries, wet acid ones that had to be recharged at the local garage. All programmes were from the BBC and there were no music or commercial programmes. There were certain programmes each week which one didn't miss. Tommy Handley in ITMA – It's That Man Again - was a weekly favourite as was "Much Binding in the Marsh," with Kenneth Horne and Richard Murdoch. "In town tonight" was a topical Saturday evening chat show. They all had catch phrases such as Mona Lot the cleaner who told all the sad stories and then said "It's being so cheerful as keeps me going". Abbreviations such as "TTFN" Ta ta for now, which were the forerunners of texting shorthand. Kenneth Horne's "Not a word to Bessie about that"and Dudley Davenport's laugh.

I had my first passport in 1950 when I went to Nigeria. I had to have a yellow fever inoculation. We seldom travelled abroad as there was a restriction on how much currency we could take with us. During my trip to France and Italy in 1951 we had to rough it. My friend had a car but we stayed in cheap hotels. It was at the time when we were only allowed to take £50 with us, the equivalent of £300 approximately in today's money. I cashed £5 travellers' cheques, and one of these on 30th June gave me 4,840 French francs. I had six of these for the whole holiday. It was my first experience of travelling through France to the Italian border at Menton. Few people had been abroad and many had never gone far from their villages as is the case in rural France now. Most holidays were a fortnight at the sea to recharge the batteries and improve health; most of us thought of the holiday as two weeks by the sea.

My trip to Nigeria in 1950 was a one off to join Tony and Mabel. It was the first time that I had flown in an aeroplane, a Hermes Speedbird, with four propellers, which was the common means of propulsion before jet and turbo prop engines. The aircraft were flown by British Overseas Airways Corporation (BOAC) for long haul flights as distinct from the European flights by British European Airways (BEA). We stopped at Tripoli in North Africa to refuel and then flew across the Sahara Desert to Kano. The plane usually flew below the clouds so we had a splendid view of the countryside, a pleasure which we don't often have today but one which I enjoyed. My first impressions of the mud city of Kano, were the noble Hausa buglers on their camels, the minarets and the mud buildings. I was amazed at how quickly one could move from one civilisation to another.

When I worked in Belfast I had to take one week of my holiday in July when the factory closed, when all its machinery stopped, or was repaired, and there was no production. We still had clothing coupons which meant that we could only buy a certain number of essential clothes, but this gradually changed and by the time I left Cambridge, I could buy cravats and yellow ties. Most of the woollens were hand knitted and the women of the family were taught to knit from an early age. Aunt Marjorie used to knit me a pair of socks each birthday, and I had several hand knitted sweaters. As we walked everywhere, I obtained a strong pair of Veldtschoen shoes from South Africa for all occasions. They were brown, a welcome change from black shoes. Trainers were unknown, but we had white rubber soled gym shoes for tennis and squash, and heavy leather boots with nailed in studs for winter games. It could be dangerous to tackle someone if there was a loose nail and you might get an ugly scratch on the cheek. The ball was leather with a rubber tube like a tyre, and got heavy when wet. It was difficult to head or kick compared with today's plastic ball and light boots. It was remarkable that we were allowed to head such a ball. Goal posts were not padded as today. For cricket we wore white flannels, no helmets and only pads and gloves. Tennis racquets had heavy wooden frames with catgut strings, unlike the flexible and plastic light weight models which are more adaptable for the game now.

There was no central heating in most homes, and solid fuel with open fires and stoves was common practice. The stoves were large metal contraptions with mica windows in the doors, and you filled them with fuel and the metal gave off heat. Hence the fire guard at all times to prevent children being burned. We usually swam in the sea rather than in swimming pools, which tended to be open and not heated. We endured severe cold water bathing in the sea in inclement weather, which was good for the circulation. Bathing on the county Down coast could be a penance, but fun if there were a good number of you. Beaches were exciting places to be and I was always sorry to leave.

One could do very well on a little money. When I started work at £400 a year (£11,000 now) I could get a gallon of petrol for four shillings in 1952 and a smoked salmon sandwich and glass of Guinness for two shillings and threepence. By the time I was twenty, I had not washed or ironed a garment, cooked a meal, or done anything other than some washing up at Trent and cleaning my own shoes. At St Georges that was done for us when we first arrived, but the war changed all that. At Cambridge we were still served by waiters in Hall in the evening, and these were male. Women, known as bed makers, came into College to make our beds; there was a nurse and a mending lady for repairing our clothes. At Trent there was a linen room; there seemed to be plenty of women available to carry out these tasks. I had no bank account but used a post office book for drawing cash from my allowance provided by Tony. My College bills at Kings in 1952 show laundry at £2 (£55) a term, £11 tuition fee, lectures£4 room rent £12 and kitchen bill nearly £18 a term. My final bill which had to be paid before I took my degree was just under £84 (£2,400) for the term. Any bill for £2 or over had to be signed over a 2d stamp.

For holidays we mostly went to the sea and in 1949 we took over my Uncle Jack's house in Carickfergus. I bathed off the rocks at Whitehead. In 1944 Mabel took me to Derry to see Graham and Peggy who were then stationed there, and then to Drogheda to the Cowdy family. John Cowdy ran the mill and had the manager's house nearby and we were made very welcome. I had my clarinet, which was then only a simple system instrument, hired from school, and he got out his flute which he had played as a young man and we had a joyful evening. During the war we had had a holiday at White Rocks near Portrush where we bathed in the Atlantic waves and this was my first experience of staying in a hotel so we made the most of it each day despite the weather.

At my first school we wore a blazer and a school cap similar to that worn by cricketers, and carried a leather bag or satchel for our exercise books. It was cumbersome and heavy for a small boy. Our accents and pronunciation would have been different as we had not acquired the Australian habit of raising our voices at the end of each sentence. We laughed at Dr Fellowes at St Georges who talked of Know (pronounced NO) ledge and Harold MacMillan said poe-litical for political. Then there was decade with the accent on the first syllable.

We use the word tuppence instead of two P and penny (d) for pence. Half a crown, two and sixpence, was half a dollar, and a two shilling piece was a florin. It was only at Cambridge that I stopped wearing a tie everyday and dressed more informally but in the evenings we had to wear our undergraduate short gowns if we went out, so that the proctors, who were responsible for law and order, could distinguish us from the others, hence the expression town and gown. At school, it was endless gray suits and blue blazer, long socks with garters with a badge in the summer, and of course the tie, school or prefect. We also had a great coat, a heavy overcoat to be worn so the rules said when we were watching school matches. When we became prefects we were allowed to put our hands in our trouser pockets and strut around as if we owned the place. This was a terrible habit. On Sundays we wore very formal dark Sunday suits, even at Cambridge, as I have a photograph of Tony Laughton, Paul Hughes and myself standing on one of the bridges wearing these suits. In the same year, 1950, when I went to Nigeria, I wore long baggy shorts with knee length socks, which was standard dress for the tropics, nothing sloppy or short!

To meet the opposite sex one learnt to do ballroom dancing, how to hold a partner, do the waltz and quickstep, and possibly a few South American dances. In Ireland there was the Pride of Erin waltz, a lilting Irish melody, and other progression dances were the military two step and the Gay Gordons. Alan Cook recalls how he and I were sent to dancing class and given the once over by two professional lady dancers. Dances were held in private houses if they were large, mainly in the Christmas holidays or halls and there was usually a live band of two or three musicians. Paula had her birthday dance at the Golf Club in Craigavad or sometimes parties were held in the Inn at Crawfordsburn. These were formal occasions in dress and we were in black tie and the girls in long ballroom dresses. Later Scottish dancing caught on as a form of social activity and dress was more informal.

We slept in iron bedsteads, with metal springs. These were the days before sprung mattresses and the mattress was of horsehair or flock with cotton ticking. We did

28

not have duvets, but blankets usually of a heavy kind and, if you were lucky, an eiderdown. Sheets were of good quality, and linen of course in Ireland. In winter we relied on hot water bottles if you were soft, but it was generally pretty cold. We often got chilblains on our hands and feet. Most gloves were knitted, in fact sweaters, mufflers, (scarves) socks, mittens etc were knitted for us by kind relatives, and we relied very much on these to keep out the cold. The fabrics which are available today were only for the services and it took some time for them to filter down to ordinary people. It got better after Everest was conquered in June 1953.

For swimming we had open air baths or the sea. It was quite common for the whole family to go bathing in the sea at Helens Bay, Newcastle or wherever. In adulthood we have photographs of family bathing at Bexhill, Cooden Beach or Norman's Bay with my own children. We braved the cold as part of the exercise, rather than to complete a number of lengths. I always enjoyed long distance swimming, rather than the swimming sports at Trent, and being able to swim between two landmarks.

The cost of living was fairly static compared with the increases in the last few decades of the 20th century. I have bills from 1957 when Ruth and I had a small flat in a house at Larch Farm which backed on to Newstead Abbey in Nottingham, around the time Nicholas was born. We bought a 4 drawer chest for £21 and a wing chair for£27, items still in our house in France, having lasted fifty years. A shirt bought in 1962 for 2 shillings and 3pence (£30) is similar and an overnight stay in 1959 bed and breakfast £1.3s.6d.

Our main form of communication was letter writing and I have a vast collection to prove it. Together with holiday postcards this type of communication went on way into the sixties with family news and what people were up to. Comments could be quite frank and revealing. In all it was a smaller world, just recovering from war, deprivation and insularity. Change over the fifties was great in opportunity, living and culture. The family tree as illustrated on the scarf, which Joyce Cather got us all to sign, would continue to document the growth of our family, with its expanding fields of occupations and wider areas of domicile .

It was not until the sixties that we were able to get a mortgage to buy Highfields in Mansfield for £5,000 (£80,000). I believe that it is now on the market for ten times that amount. It was a large Victorian house previously occupied by builders, three floors, and several large fireplaces, so I was able to use my large allowance of concessionary coal to warm the place. It had an extensive garden, so in my thirties I was confronted with DIY jobs. Although I knew about mowing and turning over soil, I had to learn about drain maintenance, conservatory and greenhouse repair (often ending in cuts). We also had a solid fuel AGA cooker, which needed stoking, and eventually plastering and decorating some of which I did nightly before the family moved in.

Letter writing still played an important part. We had been brought up to write letters from an early age with a father overseas and at boarding school. We wrote a weekly letter home on Sundays, which my parents usually answered point by point.

It is interesting that letter writing continued into the sixties, with Tony and Mabel, Mo and Mollie, Marjorie and Doris etc and various Cambridge friends about our lives, families etc. Even Paul Hughes, who lived in Nottingham, would write a postcard saying let's go to this or that. News of the children's progress was through correspondence and visits to Ireland and holidays. I still have a collection of letters at this time. It must have been a gradual change to telephone calls and a more instant and spontaneous form of keeping up with the news. The letters when I read them again show a lot of interest in the growing family, advice, comments which we don't do now, in the age of e mails.

During the war we had attempted to become self sufficient by keeping rabbits and hens to supplement our meat ration, a pastime which today would be regarded as eccentric. However 'dig for victory' was the popular slogan encouraging us to grow our own. it was the culture of the period. Sadly we grew too fond of the rabbits and also the chickens to kill and eat them.

We never seemed to complain, but took the restrictions of the war in our stride and faced the consequences of austerity as being part of the price we had to pay for victory. Ration Books carried on for all my time at Cambridge.We kept our store of jams and butter etc and gave in our coupons for eggs and milk.

Nor were we very PR conscious. Do when he joined up in the war described his occupation as merchant although he owned and ran the business. Tony described himself on my baptism entry as Colonial Service Official. A modest description.

CHAPTER 6

Regale Collegium

It was during a preliminary visit in spring 1948 that I became excited about going up to Kings. Vice Provost Donald Beves, who was a governor at Trent invited me to see the annual production of the Marlowe Society which was "Troilus and Cressida." The ambition stayed with me all through the disappointing summer when I was suffering from tubercular glands and was hors de combat. I studied during my convalescence, with a newly graduated historian from Selwyn, and I went up to take the scholarship in December 1948. The Tutor, Patrick Wilkinson, as I subsequently found out thought that I should have taken the English award because of my all round interests, but it wasn't possible. I made enough impression to be given a place on condition that I went back to Trent and took my Higher School Certificate, so no chance of a gap year but then I enjoyed school and my fellow men so I finished my career at Trent a year after most of my contemporaries had left but relishing another summer term including cricket.

Cambridge in 1949 was a combination of wartime undergraduates, two year national servicemen, and those like me who came direct from school; a wide divergence in age if one took in the post graduates, some of whom were married men and some even pushing prams as well as studying. After the war there was a determination to revert to all that had been missed but was good and nostalgic. Our speech was without platitudes. We never shook hands or talked about the weather. We were in continual conversation with each other which had to be amusing, using plenty of adverbs, and exciting. We used adjective such as splendid, a person was amazing or the expression "madly gay" to describe an occasion. It changed over the years I was there. During my first year we had Simon Raven, the rather dissolute novelist, who ran up bills in College in an Evelyn Waugh way and then got into debt in the army. His publisher managed to get him to write his "Arms for Oblivion " series of novels, keeping him writing in digs in Deal, which paid all his debts before he ended his days as a brother at Charterhouse (he had attended the school a) presumably solvent. The latter years were identified with Marc Boxer, who became the cartoonist of his generation, but at Kings was associated with mobiles and a blasphemous article in Granta. He went on to start colour supplements and develop his talent as a cartoonist. There were others such as George Plimpton from the USA who made his way in journalism.

The opportunity was there to make friends with undergraduates from other countries such as Nigeria and elsewhere in Africa. I made a particular friend of Tom Smith from Harvard, who came to London as part of the American Embassy and might have gone further but for his early death. There was John Popper from Africa, a very civilised aristocrat, and Tom Wells from New Zealand, a rare combination of an academic and sportsman, gaining blues in both cricket and rugby.   He went on to teach Miles at Clifton as did another good friend, Martin Scott.

On the games field, because of the wide age difference, one was alongside international players in both rugby and cricket.   At Grange road on Saturday afternoon, many of the leading clubs came to play the "Varsity," as the university team was known and we had several players on our team with the asterisk denoting international. There was the discussion as to who should represent the university at Twickenham and in my final year Tom Wells with whom I played at King's was the University full back. He also got a cricket blue and was in the eleven which included Doggart, May, Sheppard and Dewes. These four found their way into the England trials after a momentous match against the West Indies at Fenners in the summer of 1950. It was difficult to keep away from this ground during the home matches when time should have been spent revising for the examinations.

An undergraduate coming up in 1949 was a gentleman according to statute. Porters carried our luggage; we called each other by Christian names, even the lecturers, if not entirely to their faces. We were here to learn but in our own time. Each week I produced an essay written with a fountain pen, _a Conway Stewart if we could afford it, on folio sized paper, to be read at leisure by our supervisors (Lord)Noel Annan and others in their rooms, reclining in armchairs. The urbanity was so different from the class room. The rest of our time was for us to organise. I learnt how to run a diary, divide my time between learning, social life and sport; what lectures to attend and which_to miss. There were opportunities to hear visiting academics or resident celebrities like Nicholas Pevsner on art.

Cambridge described by E.M Forster as a receptacle for youth" (he himself was a figure at Kings, as was the legendry Professor Pigou, who when he weather improved could be seen reading in a deck chair at one corner of the lawn wearing a red scarf. In the street opposite the college there was the Copper Kettle, Copper Dive or KP, and Millers if you were rich. If you walked down the lane by Caius College to the Seeley history library, there was an old lady selling matches like someone out of a Victorian print. I can hear her voice to this day.

Most of the colleges were for men but there were the girls of our generation at Newnham and Girton Colleges. They were outnumbered and overwhelmed with so much attention. At lectures we could admire the nape of the neck in the row in front which was a feature of their emancipation from school uniform and plaits and to have their hair up. They did not bother to reveal their figures as nowadays, so it was the head and hair that first attracted me and others. I fell very early for a Newnham girl, Esther, now an author of theology and related subjects. To walk out of lectures together was an achievement. To be invited to tea at one of the colleges was special; to escort a girl to the cinema,a a concert or a play was a thrill and the envy of others. A ball? Alas I could not afford that until my final year when my partner was Anita, from the Mackie family in Ulster, then studying at Mc Gill University in Canada.

A friendly don was John Saltmarsh, who declaimed elegantly phrased sentences on economic history in a high pitched voice. His knowledge on the chapel could be entertaining and his description and miming of early ploughing indicated a sense of pleasure in all that went on around him. A product of Gresham's, I doubt whether he ever stirred from East Anglia, but he found enough there to keep his mind and research going.

My first summer was complicated by a return of my gland trouble, so my parents arranged for me to join them in Northern Nigeria for rest and recovery. It was a fascinating time for me and when I came back Saltmarsh asked me to write about it and ever after he always flattered me by recalling that essay which I still have to this day. My visit had excited my historical sense in experiencing the country as it was emerging from tribal rule to self government, and seeing the framework of the institutions.

King's was special; Collegium Regale. Wherever you looked was either the chapel or lawns. The fact that the courts were never built up with college accommodation as in other colleges made it distinct, and you looked inwards rather than outwards. In the middle was the Gibbs or Fellows building, famous for the confrontation of Wittgenstein and Popper with the poker to demonstrate self will, and in that time occupied by distinguished academics, all bachelors, shuffling abut in their dressing gowns to the few bathrooms which the College boasted. My rooms were in Webb's court on the first floor with an Aragon window looking over the court. We had coal fires so we had collect the fuel and take it to our rooms. We could have pianos or play instruments but we had to confine this to certain hours of the day as not to interrupt study. We had a bedder or bedmaker as she was called, to tidy up and we sorted out our own laundry and rations. It was an idyllic place and no wonder we didn't want to leave. Kings was a very self contained college. In sport we had our own tennis and squash courts. Musically we had our own music society where we were encouraged to perform and Boris conducted a male voice choir, where I had my first experience of singing the Prisoners chorus from Fidelio. There was COI initials standing for Consolidated Opera Incorporate, a society which sang through Gilbert and Sullivan operas, and I recall singing the Foreman in Trial by Jury when Julian Slade, he of "Salad Days" sang the judge.

Besides music and the music in chapel, and readings, Kings gave us the opportunity to explore and experience urbanity in many different ways. The Keynes picture library was available for us to hire and for one term I had a Picasso in my rooms. Every other person seemed to be musical and the performances on Sunday evenings in Hall were varied in style and composition. I remember Alfred Deller. Donald Beves and George Rylands arranged recitals of verse and music, a genre that was to attract and inspire me and my generation. Once you were in the courts there were so many privileges available, the Fellows garden and croquet, a travelling fund for undergraduates supported by alumni who had benefitted from it, and with a bachelor Provost a room in his lodge named after Ronald Balfour, a don who had died in the war for private reading and writing.

The thing about Cambridge was that we wanted it to go on forever. "We never quite go down" as the Footlights nostalgic song went. One understands how Harold

Macmillan never wanted to go back to Oxford after the First World War. He could not bear to recall all those voices that were no longer there. It was the same with us. What did I get from Cambridge? I tried to do well at history but somehow it never took off. I should have been told to take something on and do it well but then King's wasn't a College for enthusiasms. I thought that I would discover more in the way that Ecclesiastes said "O where shall wisdom be found". I read historiography reviews in the Historical Review but was incredulous when Christopher Morris my tutor implied that you could never discount bias even from such conscientious historians as Herbert Butterfield. Noel (Lord) Annan was a powerful influence. Like a number of Kings Dons such as Patrick Wilkinson at Bletchley he had a distinguished war record and post war experience in the German Control Commission. His style was overarching history to include politics, philosophy and literature. His lectures on the social ideas of the Victorians on Saturday mornings were a sell out. He had that unmasking facility which Lytton Strachey had and which was evident in the books which he wrote namely his biography of Leslie Stephen and later his "Our Age". Perhaps he could be forgiven for letting his flair for "only connect" run away from facts as his critics were quick to point out, but it was an infectious way of working and he went on to have a role in public life in his Commission of Broadcasting, and my last conversation with him in the 1980s showed that he stuck to his views then and he put me down with one of his characteristic smiles. Christopher Morris belonged to the school of Lewis Namier, sticking to what actually happened but making it interesting nevertheless unlike other academics. John Saltmarsh, referred to above, was absorbed in the detail of economic development as was his mentor Sir John Clapham and what a find he would have been in the present time of television historians. He remained a rather quaint but lovable figure, and he once told me how he could actually walk along a beach in Norfolk in the nude for about two miles and as it was completely flat he was able to notice in time an approaching stranger and could dress before coming face to face.

If I wasn't a good historian how was it that I recall all this? It was perhaps that the dons at Kings all meant something to us and if we took anything away from those three years it as a time to get to know oneself better, ones fellow men and women, and to find out what one really liked about life. The others who went straight after school to a five or five and a half day week had little time to do that, and although they had an earlier start on us, they probably made more money and made a larger contribution to the national wealth, they missed out. For us after it all it became difficult to cram all that we liked of Cambridge into the leisure of a week end.

As the Footlights said "Cambridge stays through all your memories," Kings Parade, the backs, the chapel, and that Ackerman print which we all collected and hung on our wall. Over time they gradually faded and became as a pearl in a shell, and the ambience of the place became different from those particular years which were a time of great friendship.

In the vacations I had Cambridge friends in Ulster to pass the time with. I missed the contact of meeting up in London which so many did after going down. I did go to weddings but so many chapters closed. I made many friends and have been ever ready to return when my year comes up and to pick up where we left off. Events at King's, as it has become, offers to both Suzanne and I a continuing opportunity to visit the College and meet the present generation of that who run it. To see one's own generation achieving success has been heartening, and how thrilled I was when Peter May and Colin Cowdrey, Oxbridge young cricketers led the fight back against the West Indies in 1957.

The theatre was another feature. I failed to continue my acting by not getting picked for the Marlowe Society, but enjoyed the amateur and professional productions at the Arts Theatre. There was Julian Slade, Footlights, and John Barton and of course Peter Hall, a future Director of both plays and opera. At a small party which I gave in a long vacation term after graduation, Kim Tickell, a notable party guest, announced that he was going to see his stationmaster's son in" Romeo and Juliet" so he could not stay long. That was Sir Peter as an aspiring actor.

Although there is much else in this chronicle about friends and life at Kings, it is perhaps the love of reading and exploring the world through knowledge, which Suzanne and I now share and enjoy together, the music, the history and theology which I now have more time to concentrate on, as duties become less and my weekly reading continues and with the enjoyment and fulfilment which I learnt from King's. The College encouraged the awakening of interest in many fields including gardening and wine. Such interests remain with us.

Our year 1949 has always been a source of friends, and we kept together for at least a decade after Cambridge although our lives drifted away. Tony Newell, who features in the first essay, David Lodge whom we discovered lived near us in the Lot et Garonne, and of course John Alldis, who features in the music essay, as well as many others, who are exceptional and much loved friends.

King's is a College that welcomes you back and over the years I enjoy the occasions which they offer to non resident members and the journey is always worthwhile. Tony Laughton and I spent a weekend there and had a chance to talk about the ups and downs of our lives. I have also enjoyed introducing family and friends to the College as we are privileged to hire the Saltmarsh Rooms, yes those once occupied by my history tutor John, as a place to meet and enjoy a meal together. It's always serendipity and with the chapel services as well one comes away with a sense of continual belonging to a ever increasing circle of people which is rare to find elsewhere.

CHAPTER 7

The Lullaby of Broadway

In October 1952 I found myself in the family business making damask linen with my grandfather's cousins Courtney and his son Rives Shillington, in the outlying district of Belfast between the Falls road and the Shankhill. That walk with Kings had ended!

My task was to learn the business and its people. This consisted of a factory with a dye house, a warehouse for finished goods and stitching room for hemming. Bleaching was done elsewhere under contract. The factory had looms, yarn sorting and dressing, (but no spinning) and the cutting of jacquard cards to a graph paper design hand done in the warehouse. This was a laborious process, the cards having punched holes which dictated the weaving of the web and waft yarns to depict the damask relief design. Computer aided design will have changed all that. There was a small engineering department and a loom fixing tenter. In addition to damask table cloths, napkins etc in linen, cotton and viscose rayon were also being woven as these were now more in fashion. Some sheets and towels were also made. There was no such thing as an MBA in those days, so I was enrolled at the local Tec to learn about companies, yarns and other aspects of textiles. However my hands were so clumsy that I was never to be any good at this. My interest in heat and steam was such that I used to find my way to the boilers and talk about economisers or to the Dressing Shop where the heat and steam had to be right for the rollers to dress the yarn.

This family business always seemed more important than my grandfather's Hardware and Builder's Merchant works in Portadown. Its capital value as I remember was several times higher. Courtney Shillington lived in a large house in Strandtown known as Glenmachan Tower which gave an impression of power and wealth. I had always enjoyed his company. He was an intelligent man with wide interested in travel, music, literature, and could discuss these at the dinner table. When his wife Bertha was alive they had entertained celebrities such as Pouishnoff the pianist. He was kind to my mother and to me so I was frequently a guest there. However this facade was not long to last. The industry was in decline and it was a case of sleep walking to disaster. He was eighty and spent his time at the works doing what he must have done all his life, with no desire to change his way of working. Rives had other things to occupy his time. He was an RNVR man concerned with HMS Caroline; he had been a car racing enthusiast, and ADC to the Governor of Northern Ireland which brought him a CBE. It was a pity that they didn't sell up and put their capital elsewhere into growth and development, but I suppose with a workforce of a hundred or so they felt a duty to their employees.

The system was quite primitive compared with life today. On pay day we were individually called to the office of the Accountant Mr McCrea and he would carefully count out our money and hand it over to us with a slip showing what had been deducted for pension and insurance. He was a very careful man. He had a Wolsey car which he only used on Sunday when he drove his sisters who kept a sweet shop, in Belfast where Mo used to buy her sweets, to somewhere in the country for tea. That was one of the advantages of Belfast in those days when you could get out of town and into country or coast quickly for sailing. I recall some pleasant evening after work getting to White Rock for sailing in a summer evening. The giving of cash in envelopes had its dangers, as I member a hard luck story of one of the lower paid workers throwing a fiver on the fire thinking it had been taken out of the envelope and the fiver was most of his earnings.

Workers lived in houses front to front and back to back in the street where the factory was or in adjacent streets. It was in between the Falls, Catholic quarter and the Shankhill and Sandy Row where the Protestant Orange halls predominated. It later became well known to the army in their patrols. I found them all decent people and generally honest and content with their lot. There were families and connections all round, as in most of Ireland. For instance the chief designer had a brother in the Warehouse and, when he died, I took his place looking after export orders. Some of them went on working well into their eighties. To begin with I used to end my day by having a Guinness on the Falls Road and buying a specially ordered copy of the Times. I must have looked like a special agent as I sat in a Falls Road pub, in my duffle coat as I waited for my bus back to Derriaghy

Cousin Courtney, known as the "Governor," still ran the business. Although in his eighties, his chauffeur Scott, who was also the gardener, drove him to work five days a week. He had worked there all his life and in the early days had cycled from Glen Machan. The post would be opened by the managers and he would preside over this twice a day and allot the tasks. It was a true example of the protestant work ethic, which he never changed or adapted to the modern world of telephone, teleprinter or speedier communication. Orders emanated from agents in various countries and from offices in England staffed by employees. This was where I had hoped to end up, but the business deteriorated rapidly and at the end of 1956 it was redundancy for me and several others. But this was not before I had learnt a lot about the running of a business, responsibility for orders, dealing with delays and making acquaintances with agents and others along the way and sharing common interests. There were a number of families engaged in this trade who had benefited from the war and the quotas of orders available on an equal basis but, as the market declined and became more competitive, only the best remained. After Broadway went into voluntary liquidation, most of the others also failed and that generation of families businesses lost out unless they saw an opportunity of taking up other enterprises which the modern world demanded.

Today, I am told, that double damask is only woven in Banbridge by the Fergusson mill and that Andrews in Comber have moved all their machinery to Hungary, where now the linen is made, and only marketed in Ireland or through the internet.

It is easy to be wise after the event and I was not able to influence or change the conservatism of the operation. Looking back on it, I had learnt on my feet about the detail and practical side of keeping a business going. I was never given the chance to do any paper work or write reports, a skill that as a BA graduate from Cambridge I should have been able to use and not just kept on the shop floor for four years. My friend from Cambridge, Ken Alexander, who spent time in Belfast in his family business, said that to go into business one neede to forget that one had ever been to Cambridge. Things are so different now, when intelligence is much more important than just being a spare pair of hands around the place trying to be useful. But that was the way it was then. Perhaps I felt aggrieved about this but there was a reluctance to let me use my intelligence or learn some of the principles behind the business such as costings and margins. It was difficult to find employment again, as potential employers were suspicious as to why a young man with ability had got the push, and I wasn't given a reference. A few years later, because of sector decline, the business went into administration, not a nice fate for a family firm.

I had several interviews with textile companies in England. One company in Derby even indicated what I might do, but a takeover was brewing so there was no recruitment that year. I was made an offer for a place by a company in Liverpool but the confirmation of a second interview with the Coal Board caused me to turn it down, and that was the end of any skills which I had acquired in textiles.

Courtenay Shillington, always a friend, kept in touch, but eventually moved and spent time in hospital before his death. Glenmachan Tower the flagship was sold and today it is a home for the elderly attached to a Church of Christ which has been built on Scott's vegetable garden where we used to gather raspberries. It still commands a view across he Lough where we used to watch air displays from what now is Belfast City Airport or George Best as it is called. What has happened to the other families the Ewarts, the Greeves, Forrests and other Strandtown families? C.S. (Jack) Lewis is remembered for his books and may have made those woods off Glenmachan Road a part of the background for his Narnia stories. Some day more of this may be chronicled. There is a record of his youth in Strandtown and I too remember, as he did, the chemist Horatio Todd, who gave me my first pet, a budgerigar.

I did make some good friends during that time, in particular John and Lawrence Bryson, the former a keen cellist, both of whom worked for their family firm. Lawrence married Hilary who became a good friend of Ruth when she was there and we continued to se Lawrence in Mansfield. Through them I met Noel Colisson a trainee with the tobacco firm Gallahers, with no Irish connections, but we both enjoyed trips to Strangford Lough on Saturday mornings to see the flight of the geese, a dangerous pursuit as one could get stranded in the mud. Estuaries all over Ireland are wild and one can find the unexpected in them. Many people return to them and continue to enjoy them. We had a holiday on Strangford when the children were young, and went back with Edward, Marianne and their children to Castle Ward and Portaferry, seal watching along the shore.

It was a chance encounter with Kenneth (Joe) Alexander, a member of the cast of the 1952 Footlights "Tip and Run", whom I had met at Cambridge, which led to us sharing Hilda's flat at Derriaghy and having a lot of fun together. This larger than life entertainer, who like me was finding his way in industry in one of the subsidiaries of his family business Tennants, went on to have a successful career in the family chemical company.

I left Ulster feeling disappointed and that I had lost out compared with my Cambridge contemporaries, all now going up the ladder. I was glad to get away from what I regarded as a backwater. Later when the civil rights issue came I saw Uncle Graham on Television, trying to control the situation,and I realized what I had missed. Meeting him regularly after he became Chief Constable and was knighted in 1974 I was kept up to date with his experiences and the unfortunate way in which different governments failed to understand Northern Ireland and let the people down. The appalling losses of life in the Royal Ulster Constabulary, some 300,000, affected him deeply. (10)Such losses and hardships borne by the families of the province were like that of another war and one can only admire the resilience of the community as it rises above its hatred and comes to terms with reconciliation.

The Shillington family continued to play their part in the difficult period that followed. I recall a letter I had from my cousin Colin Shillington, when he was awarded the CBE, in which in reply to my comment that he was the third generation of the Shillingtons in public life, said "one of the problems of the Province is that too many families have criticised from the touchline and not played a responsible role." He above all carried the idea of service into the third generation and in his modest and quiet way is the successor of his father and grandfather.

I had my Ulster heroes who had flourished in the wider world, such as the poet Louis MacNeice, whose words "In the beginning was the Irish rain" resonate with me and bring back memories of those whitewashed cottages which are so much a part of that landscape. Another heroine is Helen Waddell, the happy Presbyterian girl, who found such delight in the medieval poetry of France and its association with the pilgrims from St Comgall's at Bangor. Finally, of course, C.S.(Jack) Lewis and his wide contribution to literature. All these seemed to find something similar to what I did about Ulster and today I am proud to call myself an Ulsterman although it took me some time to come to terms with it. I remember well 1948 when Ireland won the Triple Crown and most of the team, such a Jack Kyle, were not only from Ulster, but were Queens University men whom Sidney knew.

---

¹⁰ *For the full story of the RUC The Fateful Split by Chris Ryder Methuen Publications Ltd 200*

CHAPTER 8

E Tenebris Lux

April 1956 was the occasion when I crossed the threshold of Hobart House in Grosvenor Place, the beginning of my career in the coal industry. Pat Mac Ilvenna, a wartime colonel was in charge of recruiting gradates and although I had had experience in another field, I was selected for an interview panel lasting several days, including dining with senior people in the industry, and giving them a chance to observe the candidates and their capabilities.

The road to this encounter had been difficult one with several false starts and near misses with other textile companies, so it was with trepidation that I reported to Mansfield in the middle of the summer of 1957 The office was run by a quietly spoken and gentle man called Harold Sherwin who was highly intelligent but owed his position to diligence first spotted at the Sunday school in Derbyshire where his colliery company did most of their recruiting for the non mining staff.

It was to be a summer of regaining confidence as I got to know some of the managers of this industry whose lifestyle was superior in every way from those whom I had left behind in Belfast. Motor cars were regular for most, and they were welcoming and ready to accept me and for me to learn about the industry and its dichotomy between public industry and the private sector who did most of the distribution and selling. This civility was apparent with working in all the functions from I to surface, wagon loading, colliery office, science laboratory.

For this I was allocated to the Edwinstowe Area comprising the cream of Nottinghamshire pits and turning some ten million tons annually. My mentor was Hal Dunstan, who had served in the war and worked with Lancashire collieries. His assistant was Edward Wilkinson, a Reptonian and Sherwood Forrester, slightly younger than I and I became, as he now calls it, his apprentice. We were and still are good friends. I greatly appreciated those months with them as part of my "Cook's Tour" of the industry and became attached to the East Midlands making many friends whom I still see. It had a civilised and appreciative ethos about it which some of the other divisions reviled as being too gentlemanly.

I arranged to have basic training as a miner along with other new recruits for which, after three weeks ,I received a certificate signed by the then Minister of Power, Lord Mills. So to add to the language of textiles which I had acquired at Broadway, I now learnt about pit bottom stint, long wall face, stable hole, dinting and of course snap. This enabled me to follow the conversations of mining engineers, planners, when we discuss seams, quality control, and items of mine management with the more qualified mining engineers, directors and others in the industry.

After some months in the East Midlands whose coat of arms was black diamonds and the motto "e tenebris lux" I had a stint at headquarters at Hobart House. Here I found that there were jobs expected to be filled by trainees, such as taking minutes at Board meetings, drafting letters, acting as secretary to committees, and other tasks that fell to the Secretariat. This was run on Civil Service lines by Cyril Roberts, a cultivated Etonian. Others in his staff included another Etonian Tom Nicole with whom I was to have dealings later when working with the Stoke Orchard team. One got to know at first hand the members of the board, the part time members (non execs) and get a feel for policy discussion. I had the experience of hearing the board discuss Harworth Colliery in Nottinghamshire where I had been only weeks before. A great friend and much admired colleague at this time was Colin Cowe, the Deputy Secretary, who spent much time with me and taught me so much. He could have been a mentor but his career was cut short by a car crash resulting in brain damage, so the rest of his life was spent on less pressurised work

Other mentors were John Menheneott, another colonel from the war and someone who had been in railways before the war, and was to rise to some height in the industry by sheer hard work and application. Much respected for his straightforward honesty, charm and good humour he was a thoroughly decent man. The other was Derek Ezra who typified that generation, and whose chairmanship of the industry and subsequent appointments was to be part of my life for a long time to come.

The current management structure was to split up the department and give both seniors and juniors responsibility for their own part. Thus accountancy was cost and financial, personnel pay and conditions and training, capital expenditure or revenue, panning or production and so it went on. This split taught one to be responsibility for the budget; the expenditure and the targets and ingenuity of running one's own show. In marketing we were divided between domestic and industrial, road and rail transport, wholesale or retail, and here were departments for utilities, shipping and technical. The whole thing was co-ordinated by a departmental secretary reporting to the Marketing Director. He was Norman Fricker as well turned out a man as you could find, hair beautifully shampooed and curled, immaculate suits .One wondered if he had been anywhere near a colliery or handled the black stuff. He could be charming and he could be sarcastic. He demanded loyalty and he rewarded it handsomely. He preferred his staff to be gentlemen or to touch the forelock. His company house was Steetley Hall in north Nottinghamshire. He had family in the coal trade, the part which had not been nationalised so he had a foot in both camps.

We were a cheerful office and although run to strictly rules by Harold Sherwin whom was teetotal, there were others lie one Dudley Pexton who believed that the best way to get to know your customers was over a drink and here was a good pub across the road at Mansfield Woodhouse where we were situated partly in a house and partly in prefabs. The office had an accounts department which were responsible for invoicing the sales of the region and for producing statistics. I am told that the type of hip which we had in those days was equivalent to the chip which we now have in a musical Christmas or birthday card so there was a lot of manual work. Contracting was also a laborious business, matching the coal output from the collieries to the contracts asked for by the merchants. This went across other parts of the country and transport costs came into this, as well as preferences and the amount of domestic coal was getting less year by tear as machine mining broke up the cola into even smaller pieces.

There was an idea, which I chose to back, that this laborious exercise, which was usually done after hours every three years when we sat down and added and subtracted with substitutes and alternatives could be done more easily by computer. Don Catchpole a scientist, then heading a movement for application for computers to management, devised a programme for us and we duly completed the exercise in double quick time. The computer had done things which we couldn't understand and we had an embarrassing interview with the Marketing Director Bill Burton, suspicious of the operation, who asked questions which we couldn't answer and only the computer could. We were so nearly right and on time compared with other offices that it was disappointment to be criticised by our own people. However Don came to the rescue and the system which we had piloted became the standard for future contracting.

Somehow I fitted into this system and became selected for new and emerging initiatives Three of these stand out.

The first was when I was considered too inexperienced for the job I coveted and was chosen to start and set up a retail shop in Mansfield a post which I would ultimately hand over to someone else when he was trained. The idea was to have a front in the High Street which would sell coal and advice on solid fuel heating for the residents of Mansfield and district. The local trade were up, in arms and thought that we would take trade from them. They criticised the expensive site as did the builders merchants. It did give the industry a front with the local community and the idea was to promote rather than compete. I stayed in this job for about six months and we recruited some good people. I had experience in what it was to be a shopkeeper, look after cash, and lock up and all that which happened without incidence. The only problems were with our female staff that were picked for their charm, one of them going so far as to have an illegitimate baby and the other having an affair with a member of the senior magagement.

Following this in about 1960, the Coal board decided to embark on a programme of publicity and sales promotion, and had selected a senior person J.S Williams to run this. John Menheneott and I went to the meetings in London and came back with a host of things to do each month. These included going into advertising in major papers, introducing fuel technologists, running promotions about domestic heating with coal in local communities through show houses with builders. Competition with oil was becoming great as prices and deals on futures were made with customers particularly in the industrial market.

One of the features was to run a campaign with leading industries that relied on coal for their business. We did this with Raleigh the Nottingham bicycle manufacturer, and I found a lead with one of the breweries in Burton on Trent. This involved a very heavy day of selling at Burton with visits to the sample room but in the end we got our advert and our local companies featured well in this campaign. For this I was allotted on assistant but when they came to value the job as was the way, it was rated at two grades higher than I was. With a declining industry a suitable person was found, Chris Perry, not long to go for retirement, and he was given plenty of staff which I wasn't, but he had the experience of a growing department. John was very kind in telling me that it wasn't good for my career to be solely and specialise in publicity, so off I went to do more commercial work

The third was after a reorganisation when I was nominated to cover bituminous coal on the domestic side of the business. Our research team under Bill Kaye at the Research laboratory in Stoke Orchard had come up with a way of burning coal smokelessly and had developed a glass fronted room heater with a back boiler similar to those which were being put into council houses and which burned a smokeless fuel. The research people needed a site to test this. Our domestic technical staff knew that one of the miners estates near Chesterfield were to go smokeless and would lose their concessionary coal which they piled on their fires, so this seemed a good place to try this. The result was a series of unrelated problems which occupied my time and worry, during 1967 and 68.It brought about my first meeting and subsequent interview with chairman Lord Alfred Robens, meetings with other politicians such as Eric Varley ,Dennis Skinner of Bolsover We were helped in the political scene by Tom Nicole, with whom I had worked before, and with his inimitable urbanity and savoir faire, which kept us from failing, and above all a lasting and fulfilling friendship with Bill Kaye, whose team at Stoke Orchard had develop the heater and whose knowledge friendship and support was essential in the time of crisis.

By choosing this estate, which was Wimpey No Fines built, the change of heating caused condensation and a number of problems with tenants who were not adept at running a sophisticated heater? Sometimes they over heated it which resulted in burning out the fire bars but luckily one of the engineers at Stoke Orchard had foreseen this and replacements were on hand. In addition to this field trial problem, there was opposition to packaged coal replacing bagged coal which because it was concessionary the miners could sell on their additional allowance. We also came up against the communists in the pit who fought against this imposition. Luckily we had some reasonable housewives on the estate who welcomed the idea of radiators and a cleaner environment in the end we managed after a great deal of management time to calm it own. The Housewarmer was installed in another estate which although we had similar problems the main one was with the local clean air inspector who did not believe the test record of the emissions and hence the interview with Richard Adams, the author of the best selling Watership Down, at the department of health, where the complaint was made. In the end the prototype was improved and manufactures elsewhere and became a standard appliance. I had the experience of having a team around me whom I learnt to value and manage according to their skills. Bill Kaye's team also did well and between us we kept the thing going and remain friends to this day. He and his daughter Alison have been to stay with us in France

Before all this I had had my time as a Sales District Manger or Nottingham, had several visits to staff college at Chalfont to learn about Management by Objectives and even been there for an interview for going on the staff, which happened again later. I was also picked out o go on Sales Analysis course an American system which Alfred Robens said we needed, and when in Nottingham was asked to join the Junior Chamber of commerce and I became President in 1967 and joined a committee of the Chamber of Commerce as deputy chairman.

When I look back on these years I see plenty of smiles and laughter. Malcolm Edwards who was my boss during the housewarmer time seemed always to come out smiling and had tremendous courage and tenacity when he needed to hold his corner. We got on well. I frequently meet Edward Wilkinson, John Hallam, Paul Glover and Bill Kaye. The senior team at Mansfield Woodhouse, whom I had known were retiring, and the establishment was changing and being amalgamated with the West Midlands so it was good to get away to London, where a new chapter would begin.

I had appreciated the experience of being in the East Midlands coalfield and working near the coal face for a time at one of the areas, where life was informal and I got to know the management team and their professional and technical abilities. The network of an area was like a company, producing about 1 million tons, accountable for quality, proceeds, and profit. Production rubbed shoulders with finance, and as marketing we interfaced with most of the others, except for industrial relations, which was to play a great part in the periods that followed but then it was an uneventful time. We almost had a rail strike and I recall emergency meetings then when our transport arrangements had to be switched to road haulage to avoid disruption. The mining engineers were a good breed of men, many of whom had come up the hard way with degrees at the universities. They frequently found it easy to take up other jobs in management, but the system was for a delegated production focus, with area and group mining, and other non mining matters were left to the chief clerk and the specialist departments when needed. This happy band had a traditional Christmas party and pantomime where no side and a sense of humour was essential.

At the end of my fourth decade, which had been spent in Nottinghamshire, I had had bought my first house. Although having no professional qualification, I had been to staff college and been trained in various skills, had had plenty of experience in different jobs, got to know the area well and to have a liking for it. The conditions and opportunities at this time were good in this industry, attracting able mining engineers and managers, many of whom stayed for a lifetime. I had developed a mutual respect by them during my first temporary post in an area, when we had to cope with a possible rail strike. As I made my way to London from Nottingham station on Monday mornings I realised that my life was changing, but I was going where I had always wanted to be. I had a background of experience of the industry, a reputation for commercial acumen, some administrative experience and had managed people in a team. All this I hoped would stand me in good stead in the coming years working with David Broadbent whose skills I came to admire and from whom I was to learn much.

CHAPTER 9

Accentuate the positive

1970/1 was a changing time both domestically and professionally. Suzanne and I got together and I was offered the opportunity to work in London. I joined Special Projects, a department reporting at high level and run by David Broadbent. David was an engineer, qualified in all the disciplines of the profession, and with a lot of cheek. He had a short fuse when things didn't go his way, and was quick to name scapegoats whom he would continue to persecute. If things went right he smiled so happily and was so over-generous to you that it was embarrassing. During the years we got on well together; he had a taste for good food and where to find it, so that was a bonus.

The outgoing chairman, Lord Alfred Robens, had led the coal industry with purpose and dignity, giving up a career in politics to do so. His work for the industry is recorded in two books "Ten Year Stint" and "Human Engineering." He became a byword for management and he made his role as chairman significant within the industry and elsewhere. He was on the court of the Bank of England. I only had one occasion to meet him in his office, with several others who were senior to me, but he wanted to know my personal views and how we should go about things. He then backed me up. After coal he did many things in public life, and one of these was to raise funds for Westminster Abbey. At his memorial service, in the Abbey, there was already a stained glass window for him depicting colliery winding gear and as, the service finished, the Grimethorpe Colliery Band played "I did it my way," a fitting finale for the lad who had started life in the Cooperative Society and finished in the House of Lords.

Our team of some eight was drawn from several disciplines. I was asked to take on the Immingham project, a joint loading and shipping terminal on the Humber, working with British Steel. It was run by a colleague whom I had known for some time, Geoff Ashmore. It proved an interesting time for me, with trips to the Humber, joint meetings with the contractors on construction, British Steel executives, briefing of different board members and picking up non-technical issues as they arose. One of these was rating. Off shore terminals were new to Britain and, although this one was situated in a dock area, the loading was done outside towards the sea. We had a large rating demand which we fought and negotiated, but eventually we had to consult Counsel in chambers. I was deputed to accompany the lawyers to the chambers of David Widdicombe the expert on rateable values. The cash register was ticking over as I was asked to explain what exactly the Immingham Bulk Terminal was. Showing Mr. Widdicombe a map, I pointed out to him what it was, where it went and what happened. I suppose I was the expert witness. The presentation went on to rate demands and the like and eventfully we were dismissed to find out later that our demand had been reduced from £100,000 to nearer £30,000, a great morning's work.

This was the start of Derek Ezra's time as chairman, when there was beginning to be an interest in the environment, so David asked me to collate the good and the bad, positive and negative, working with the various departments. Environment was a sensitive issue with the mining engineers who had just experienced the disaster at Aberfan, when the spoil tip had collapsed and overflowed into the local school. However there was a tale to tell with the Opencast Executive whose track record in reclamation of derelict sites was second to none. Bearing in mind the example of Stoke on Trent, where a derelict site had been turned into a country park, Robens offered their expertise to the government to clear up industrial dereliction elsewhere in the country. However they decided against it.

One morning I was asked to sit in on a meeting, at which the chairman was Peter Parker, someone whom I was to regard and admire for his inspiration and leadership for many years to come. From this meeting came a group of industrialists and business people determined to show the better side of industrial development. This was a movement started by the Civic Trust, who hoped to benefit from consultancy in transferring their experience in town improvements to the industrial landscape of the country. Our group felt otherwise. If some of them were capable of doing it themselves, why not go on and show the country what could be done with the industrial muscle and knowledge which they had. With Peter Parker in the lead, we established a group able to give both financial and professional resources to make this work. The first thing was to find out what was happening. A Welsh journalist, John Gay Davies, told us the way to do this was, as he had done while an editor of a Welsh paper, when they wanted to increase circulation by having a beauty contest. Get everyone to enter his wife, daughter, sister, and the next year the readers will say "if she can get the prize so can I." That is what happened. We all found projects for the first year. A whisky distillery in Scotland had designed their building in Scottish traditional style, and Shell had created an oil depot in Glasgow which was barely visible to the public. The following year BP was determined to show what they could do and a series of similar industries, when approached, were determined to show their good practice as a means to support their planning prospects. The Civic Trust remained with us and their two stalwarts Michael Middleton and Peter Robshaw stayed the course and we found much common ground. We were a help to them in strengthening their industrial support. I was excited to be in on this as a junior from the start and got to know the assessors, John Wells Thorpe, an architect, who later turned up as chairman of a neighbouring health trust, Eric Usher of the Electricity industry, David Lawrence of the Railways Property Board and many others whom I could list. The latter became a great friend, and we had common interest in church architecture. Under his guidance the competition expanded and the quality was sustained. Our presentations became an annual event at the Royal Society of Arts, when we invited government ministers to present the awards. As a trio we worked well and supported by a growing number of industrialists and professionals, whom Peter invited to lunches, we did our bit to further the momentum of what we had started in 1975. We carried on in this amateur and British way for many years reaching and overcoming each crisis of existence in turn. Peter, who went on to become chairman of British Rail and received his knighthood, was a friend until his untimely death. His annual Christmas cards of drawings by William Blake were cherished and his courteous letters with messages about meeting, as on occasion we would snatch a brief encounter at the Garrick Club or breakfast at the Savoy. His Oxford contemporary, Shirley Williams, said of him in her autobiography, that he didn't walk but he bounced and he was like when he came to meetings. In one sentence he could reveal his inner thoughts and have you with him. One could not fail to be fired by this man and I was saddened by his sudden death on holiday in Greece. Among the many tributes to him the Times printed a tribute from me in which I wrote about his pioneer work in considering the environment as a company issue "bringing together in a common purpose, management both public and private, trade unions and the professional institutions. Much of what he encouraged has been enshrined in management education and the mission statements of many companies, but his early spotting of environment as an issue to be talked about in public was courageous and far sighted." David and I attended his memorial service along with his family, royalty and many of the causes which he had promoted.

David Broadbent's department continued to be a flexible instrument for taking on immediate tasks. The technical consultancy was done by my colleagues and I concentrated on the administrative, commercial and other sides of his work, which brought me into contact with several departments including legal, insurance, staff for personnel and the central secretariat. Particular allies were Denis Barber and John Loudon of finance, with whom we had many sessions on accountability. Consultancies with Rev Lord Sandford, Wayland Young (Lord Kennet), came my way. The system was easy to work provided there was a budget. We did this also for the Nationalised Industries Overseas Group, which was set up by a seconded civil servant Harry Slater. Above all there were the meetings in Brussels with other industries. Over the years my circle of colleagues was growing and my interests were expanding both in the country and abroad as the working world became wider.

Establishing publicity for environment achievement in the industry was difficult. The coal industry had been guilty of years of waste tipping on the Durham beaches. This was a constant source of criticism, so perhaps the less said about that the better. David Broadbent took a different view. He considered that we should be more up front in publicity. In our travels around we had found many good examples of people doing good work which had gone unrecognised. For instance we came upon some derelict land reclamation work at a place called Hetton le Hole, in the North East where the pit heap had been transformed into a playground for children. We decided to enter it for a Times Conservation Award, and I with the local town clerk prepared the citation. To our delight this project was selected for the top award and was given publicity in the Times. A rather surprised mining engineer, Sam Potts, accompanied me to the presentation and received a handsome shield. It was what followed that was surprising. The next morning there was a visit from Biddy Baxter who was the producer of the children's Blue Peter programme. I was invited to show her our model of the project which was in my office. She was a thoughtful person with roots in the north, so she immediately asked questions and started thinking. The upshot was that the model went to the BBC and children were invited to submit drawings of their local wasteland and what they would like to see which would transform it. The result was unbelievable and we received well over 30,000 drawings, from which we were asked to select the best for a short list to be judged on television, followed by a special party for the winners. Derek Ezra and the President of the Miners Union, Joe Gormley, were to be the front people for this but Derek sadly became ill and another board member deputised. We had a good evening at the BBC and eventually the winners were entertained by us at Wakefield, presented with miners' helmets and saw the draglines at work on an opencast site. This whole experience which I handled was most revealing and it showed the variety of things which were going on in our industry, which the public needed to see to compensate for the darker side.

David's team became the company for carrying out coal research under the International Energy agency (IEA). We establishing a fluidised bed plant in Grimethorpe. This was a form of combustion, creating a fluid at high temperature and taking off the cycle running of the gasses to drive a turbine which could be done at greater efficiency than conventional power, because of the combined gas cycle. The snag was the high temperature of the waste for disposal and the scaling up of the plant. We did this with the United States and Germany as partners, which was an experience in international relations, and my job was to pick up the non technical aspects of the project, legal, insurance, pensions and to get permits for suitably qualified staff from overseas and the various related industries in the UK. When David was in charge, we were accustomed to working together, but on his retirement I learnt to work with Richard Jack a secondee from the Electricity industry, a metallurgist and scientist some 15 years younger.

We had a hair-raising time when our American sponsors decided to pay a snap visit to the plant in Grimethorpe, and insisted on using their own US Congressional plane rather than the train to Doncaster. We had to arrange flight procedures with both Heathrow and the local Yorkshire airport. That meant only three hours in Yorkshire including local travel. When the plane arrived on the runway the portable gangway was too low for the large aircraft, so we had another delay. I stood side by side with the local officer, who, when I started to panic, said don't move it's not our problem. The US Congressional jet had not issued instructions to the landing team.

I was fortunate, thanks to David and Peter Parker, to continue with the Environment Awards and gradually in Peter's words to be the Ark of the Covenant. Assessors changed as did chairman when David retired and we got to know number of enthusiasts and past winners as the movement took off. David Lawrence succeeded as chairman and the three of us had a very fruitful time together as photographs of us show. My various secretaries all told me that they particularly liked that side of my work, and Julie Paul was able to join us at Harrogate when we gave the awards at the CBI conference, Michael Howard was Secretary of State, when my cousin Anthony received an award on behalf of Redland. As Peter and I walked back to our hotel, we talked of many things in our lives and the following morning we had a Times Supplement at the breakfast table, well organised by my BITC friend Alex Macdonald. We had travelled far since 1975.

Working with David Broadbent when Derek Ezra was chairman introduced me to working abroad. After the UK joined the Common market we became part of Centre Europeennes Entreprises Publiques (CEEP) the European organisation for public and nationalised industries. We took it in turn to go to meetings and I found myself on the environment and regional policy group. We were exploring the Brussels edifice and finding our way into many offices from Commissioner downwards at a time when we were new boys. I made friends with the Italians and in particular, Duccio Valori, an English speaker, lover of our country and we had fun working together. His company was a conglomerate in energy and his chairman, Pietro Sette, wanted to meet Derek Ezra, so we staged a conference at Hobart House with interpreters which we hosted. We had meetings in Rome and Dublin with the Irish who organised suitable places to eat, which was always a requisite of our meetings. For this I was offered a course in French to improve my linguistic ability which I was grateful to accept. As well as working with Duccio, with whose family we continue to be friends, we also got to know the other nationalised industries and arranged a tour for people from the Commission to see how we in the UK industries dealt with regional policy issues such as land improvement, miners' housing, redevelopment and community interests. It was all fun and at a time when the Community was less structured than today.

An opportunity to travel to Israel came in the late seventies. We had been working with Michael Sieff and the Anglo Israel Trade committee and, because of David's illness, I was asked to accompany them on their tour of Britain. This was done with the help of the electricity industry, our rail friends, and major coal users such as Alcan in Northumberland. The Israel Ports Authority was interested in importing coal and organising a coal-fired power station. I took them around Britain to see various forms of transport and loading, which included Immingham, and was, invited back to see possibilities at Haifa, Hadera and Askelon where already there was traffic in fluorspar. I enjoyed the visit greatly and on my afternoon off I managed to get to Jerusalem, strangely enough on the day the Pope died and the flags were a half mast. I walked the Via Dolorosa and the Mount of Olives, returning to my hotel in Tel Aviv and was taken out to dine in Joppa by my host the Chief executive of the ports, and we ate looking out over the Mediterranean, and philosophising on the common characteristic of our cultures, Christian and Jewish, the architecture, art and customs.

During this trip I experienced one of the most embarrassing situations in my life. We were discussing things around a table and I was being addressed as Mr Shillingford. To make things more informal I said "don't you think we know each other well enough to use Christian names" there was a pause and I recollected what I had just said, but a smile from Rahiv restored the status quo. However I am frequently haunted by this incident and my lack of tact and respect to Jewish friends

I spent ten years working with David and we became a good team. There were times when I wondered whether I should move on and at one time Peter Parker was being considered for an overlord job and needed staff. We knew that the outlook for coal was such that there was little future, and because of the strikes, the shape of the industry was to change. However we were encouraged to look for diversification among the other things going on in the world and we were consulted at a high level. David believed in being footloose, which nearly led to our downfall, as we were not a department, but we survived. Working with him, I learnt about visual presentation. Before the days of computers we had a draughtsman Doug Ogle, who would quietly listen to what we were trying to put over and then go away and draw it as a visual. We developed the energy gap curve or graph and several other things which became our trademark. I was to use this technique when working for BESO but then Suzanne and I worked jointly and used a computer. It is somewhat ironic looking back at that time some thirty years ago, when we all knew that in the long term it would be nuclear energy and coal had a shelf life only as insurance if the planned development didn't happen. It still hasn't and now the emphasis is on renewable wind and solar power, although there are power stations on the Trent , coal fired and operated by overseas utilities needing to be replaced by something more than just renewable alternatives but when?

What of the National Coal Board and those who worked in a nationalised industry? To some we were suspect but our rewards were less than the private sector and our work load as hard. The public sector demanded a code of conduct and with it went responsibility for large slices of investment. For those who chose to break the rules there could be temptations leading to consequences such as jail. Alfred Robens had given us purpose and he set our sights for the big approach which went down well with his peers, whom he addressed frequently, and he was on the court of the Bank of England. Some of us may have been left wing idealists who found working in the public interest more conducive to their background, while others wanted an easy life. Yet there were many who worked long hours without the greater rewards which could have been theirs elsewhere. Some took advantage of foreign travel and milked the system, but they were few. Criticised eventually for being too consensus minded and too close to the unions, it was a Conservative ex minister Lord Chandos (Olive Lyttleton) whom I heard advising managers in the 1960s to leave negotiation to the chairmen and leaders of the powerful unions. They were the generation of the war and their union counterparts were probably former comrades in arms so there was a certain trust, and beer and sandwiches at Number 10 was the ultimate. Margaret Thatcher disliked us all. If you were any good you wouldn't be working here she had said, although her husband was quite content to, take on a chairmanship of a subsidiary. Who else in the country knew about coal mining, steel making or running railways? If you couldn't respect the professionals who had been doing the job then who could you respect? Since privatisation and my meetings with former colleagues, it appears that expertise is what counts and it now seems that more coal will be needed, pits are to be reopened and some of the modern ways of using coal will be developed in a way in which we had always hoped. I may not live to see this but I feel sure that our somewhat discredited industry will continue on the foundations which in those years we tried to build.

CHAPTER 10

Music for a while

"Music is what matters to him most". So said my sister Paula, I am given to believe, when describing me to her friend Christine Falwasser who lived on the shores of Loch Etive. I was then approaching fifty and enjoying singing in several choirs, as well as having had something to do with their organising. I had also done some conducting and solo singing.

How did it all begin? Someone discovered, probably Tony, that I had an ear and could pitch. I can't recall exactly but it seemed natural to sit at a piano and work out tunes. Daisy was my first song with its three in a bar waltz rhythm, and swaying lilt. When everyone burst out singing in Knock Methodist Church, I sang that much to the embarrassment of the family. Mo was musical and played the piano at Ardeevin and I joined in. There was always music about me and I was quick to pick up accents as well as intervals. My family in Ireland still sing around the piano, traditional Irish songs which we all love.

Tony had been a chorister at St Paul's during the War, so he thought that I should follow in his footsteps. Our local piano tuner was deputed to train and prepare me for the voice trial. I learnt a number of easy songs with him to show the range of my voice and we chose "D'ye Ken John Peel" rather than an Irish song such as "the Flight of the Earls" for my choir trial. Mabel didn't like the city life of the boys at St Paul's, so St George's Windsor was chosen. Tony's Oxford friend Webb Jones was headmaster. As it turned out St Paul's disappeared to Truro for the war so it was the right decision.

I owed much to John Forster, who became assistant organist during the war and taught us piano. He seemed to be able to catch one's imagination about a piece and make it one's own. I remember that we played duet arrangements of Beethoven String quartets. Above all he found time to take me to the National Gallery concerts run by Myra Hess, where I heard Brahms clarinet sonatas, which I eventually learned to play.

Doc H was of course the inspiration at Windsor. He taught us how to sing without reservation and with the whole body so it gave us a sense of fulfilment rather than an apologetic side line with the voice box. He taught us phrasing and to sing phrases like the arches which we saw around us. Recently I saw Harry Christopher say just the same thing to his choir about early music. His exercises included the major sixth and the opening run of "For unto us" from the Messiah. He taught us to use the vowel O which gave him the sound he wanted from us and passed on his love of Handel in his teaching us to sing "If God be for us who can be against us." Walford Davies, one of his predecessors and then master of the Kings music, had told him that Handel would win the war for us.

I played the clarinet until after my time at Cambridge. I had reached a high standard at 15 in 1946 when there were four of us, good enough to play two movements from the Mozart Piano Quintet for wind at the school concert. After my illness in 1948 playing became difficult, but at Cambridge I played in various orchestras at College level. Boris Ord was the conductor of CUMS, and at King's, where he ran the chapel choir. I had the great honour to be asked to sing with the choral scholars of the chapel choir for a performance of "Alexander's Feast" by Handel in the May week concert of my first year in 1950. I was thrilled to wear my tails and white tie and to be invited to Boris's all night party afterwards. I sang quite a lot with him at College events and he taught us to sing with warmth and feeling. As a conductor he was able to draw something extra from us.

Music abounded in King's. I got to know Roger Gaunt, a gentle person of my own age who started a choir, in which I sang, and eventually we performed the Mozart Requiem in King's Chapel. We also set up a group of wood wind players which we called the Oliphant Society and got all sorts of pieces arranged for us to play by musicologists and we blew to our heart's content. I didn't make CUMS as a clarinettist, as there were a legion of clarinettists, but managed to find a place as a percussionist for Carmina Burana in 1952 and enjoyed the chance of playing in St Alessio by Cavalli in Girton College Garden with Thurston Dart playing the harpsichord. No doubt Raymond Leppard's future realizations of Cavalli's music was influenced by this.

All who came in contact with him owed much to John Alldis. We were contemporaries at Kings. Music came out of his personality; he just exuded it in his entire being . He drew the performance from the music which was put before him and nothing was too difficult or demanding. He invented his own explanations as he became inarticulate, when music took over, which led to laughter and sometime incredulity. He always achieved results and was acclaimed for them. I value him as a close friend. Now he is sadly crippled with a stroke, but I still find his company irresistible. John's greatest achievement was to create a choir of professional singers, just before they became soloists in their own right. The sound was stunning, the dynamic enthralling and he presented music from the baroque to the modern. His Debussy Chansons d'Hiver and Bruckner Motets were amazing when heard for the first time. He went on to teach at the Guildhall and run choirs worldwide. I was fortunate to be in the London Philharmonic choir at the time when he was the conductor. Daniel Snowman has written about these days in his book "Halleluiah." "With Shillingford as Chairman of the choir and Crabtree as MD of the Orchestra" he writes, "the collaboration flowed. There were some memorable London Philharmonic Orchestra and Choir concerts with Solti. But the Choir also sang under a variety of other conductors at this time, among them Chailly, Eschenbach, Lopez- Cobos, Conlon, Pritchard and Rostropovich." In addition to concerts we made acclaimed recordings with Boult of Elgar and Vaughan Williams sang under Sir George Solti, the delightful Bernard Haitink, and the neurotic Klaus Tenndsedt. John also organised recordings of popular choral works in 1976 with Irving Martin, a musical entrepreneur who found us a niche in the American market and with "Sounds of Glory" which had some 850,000 sales. This was followed by the Messiah with Felicity Lott, Philip Langdridge, and the London Philharmonic Orchestra which later in 2003/4 reached the classical charts. We also recorded "Star Clusters" by David Bedford, a first performance. In 1979 the choir were invited and managed to arrange finance to sing at a British festival in

Wilhemshaven in Germany. It was an experience not to be missed. As I was Chairman I was involved in the organising of the tour.

Hugh and Sheila Fovargue who lived in Battle, were good friends and after Sheila died as a result of a car crash, we continued to see Hugh, who was Edward's godfather. They had started a group of singers and were fond of music. They were keen to put their son Robert in for a choir trial at St George's and he was successful. His trainer had been Chris Bartrum, an organist in Hastings whom I got to know. He produced for me a method of training boy's voices for cathedral choirs. I looked at the options, and St John's and King's seemed the best from our home in Nottinghamshire, so as St John's was the first we put Nick in for the trial in January, at which he was offered a place. We of course accepted so then began the connection with that choir, with recordings and tours. Edward followed him and they both excelled at the school and we were very proud of their achievements, in the life of the school, both musically and on the playing field.

Years later as an adult, I took singing lessons from Arthur Reckless, who taught at the Guildhall. I was well in to my fifties and thought that it would be a short course but he kept me on for several years, going each week until he retired. He was coaching all sorts of people then including young BrynTerfel, the Welsh baritone. With him I developed a power in my voice and aptitude for presentation which, encouraged by choral conductors, was a great pleasure to me. We used to discuss singers and their foibles which was most interesting. Arthur had sung with Henry Wood; his career was interrupted by the war so he missed out on his potential. His encouragement is still with me today as I try some of the music which we did together.

T return to my own musical career, everything went quiet after University as I missed out on music in Belfast, although I remember attending a concert when the young Heather Harper, a local girl sang, "Morgen" by Richard Strauss. It was in Nottingham that through friends, Edward and Tom Pollit, I went to the newly formed Bach Choir run by David Lumsden, who had been at Cambridge with me, although our paths had never crossed. Choral singing in a large chorus had not been anything which I had done before and for the next fifteen years it was to play a great part in my life. It became my recreation and the clarinet was discarded in favour of singing. David was kind enough to use me to sing small solos such as Pilate and Peter in the St John Passion. I remember that he spent an afternoon rehearsing me in Southwell Minster and coaxing vocal technique from me necessary for a large building. This continued under his successor, Ivor Keys, who also invited me to be a soloist at the University in a piece by Purcell called "My Beloved Spake." Ivor also used me as a small part soloist, often at short notice. While other Cambridge contemporaries continued to sing together in London and elsewhere, I became a feature in the Midlands, except for a short sojourn with the Philharmonia when I was based in London, which included singing in the ever fresh recording of Belshazzar' Feast conducted by the composer.

One of the most thrilling experiences was to sing in the Tallis 40 part Motet "Spem in Alium Nunquam Habui," which Ivor Keys translated as "I hope I never have to come in on my own." Actually I did do just that, as I became a right marker in one of the middle choirs half way through the work. I took part in further performances later in Bromley Parish Church and the Festival Hall for the hundredth birthday concert of Sir Robert Mayer at which the Queen was present. This is a work which is both musical and mathematical. It builds sound upon sound, theme upon theme, an ethereal and unforgettable experience. "O nata lux" is another piece by the same composer that is to be treasured.

At Trent I had been introduced to conducting at the annual House Music competition. Part of this involved getting a group of people in the house to sing a unison song and one of us had to conduct. As Wright was not a very musical house, I found myself at a young age taking up the baton to direct my fellow pupils in the unison songs. These were usually patriotic numbers by English contemporary composers such as Roger Quilter's "Non Nobis Domine" and "This Royal Throne of Kings." Ford Ikin, our ex King's choral scholar headmaster coached us and gave me encouragement in producing an enthusiastic and inspiring sound from a group of lusty broken untrained voices. I managed to win the trophy for Wright on at least one occasion and thought no more about it.

It was in 1960 that we were asked to do something for the Sue Rider charity and carol singing was suggested. Suzanne, whom I had recently met, organised some singers and with few imports from the Bach choir such as Donald Bush and Pamela Carlson. We sang in people's homes and made a good sound together which seemed to be appreciated. We were all of an age and had some musical experience. We all enjoyed it and from this sprang the Newstead Abbey Singers,a choir which still survives to this day. We started to sing madrigals and part songs, some of which I had sung with Boris. Friends such as Tom and Sheila Kirkham, Peter and Fanny Saywell and our children's music teacher Doreen Anabel joined us. An invitation from Tom Kirkham to sing at his Masonic Christmas dinner in Mansfield led to Ozzie Storrs suggesting we gave a concert at a church in Perlethorpe in the Dukeries. More engagements followed and I found myself running a choir, finding and researching music and preparing for performance, using such skills as I had acquired. As I met more people interested in singing they joined us. Tim Bowles, headmaster of Bramcote, the prep school for Trent, was one of these. Our music took us to all sorts of places to sing. Mike and Anne Stacey and Tony and RhonaGlover joined us; their daughter is still involved. Tony Glover took over the choir when Suzanne and I left for London. Tim Bowles continued to be a good friend, and was Edward's godfather. A man with wide interests including climbing and gliding, he brought his organising skills to everything that he did. Being unmarried he threw himself into projects with remarkable energy. Before his death we used to enjoy watching cricket together.

We had our hairy moments, but in all we improved and became the only group of its kind in the area, and received invitations for concerts from many sources. Our triumph was to sing a concert in the cloisters of Newstead Abbey, from which we took our name, at the first Nottingham Music Festival in 1969. We sang music by Percy Grainger, Britten and Delius, as well as our 16th century madrigals, which we had sung on many occasions including a Son et Lumiere at Norwell. Conducting this choir was something which gave me great pleasure. I was able to continue conducting this after we moved to Kent in.

While in Nottingham I took part in Gilbert and Sullivan operas which were put on in our local church hall at Ravenshead by a very energetic and committed Margaret Williamson. She persuaded me to perform parts such as Colonel Calverley in Patience and my favourite, Sir Ruthven Murgatroyd in Ruddigore, which I relished, because I had to sing "When the Night Wind howls", and finish the performance by drinking a glass of sherry.

After moving in 1970 we both joined a choir at Lamberhurst in Kent run by Monica and William Morland. The story is related in William's book "Conductor's Progress" or "Husbands have their uses." This was an enterprising venture for a village. Monica conducted the choir for 40 years. We found ourselves singing Monteverdi, Baroque Italian, Handel's Theodora and Belshazzar, which William directed with all the drama he could muster, frequently at odds with Monica, who much preferred Bach. Tony and Mabel were also in this choir. We met Derek Watmough and Monica was able to entice Thornton Lofthouse and William McKie who lived in Groombridge to take part in her performances. These were usually followed by a tea at Court Lodge and, if you had been a soloist, which I was on several occasions, dinner at Goudhurst. At Lamberhurst we met Beryl and John Elliot and Michael and April Holland, who played the harpsichord. They were responsible for our move to Cowden in 1976. Beryl ran the Cowden Spring Choir and composed music for us, the highlight being a choral piece called "Hear Joel," in which I was the bass soloist. It was at this time that we were asked to find singers for a wedding in our church in Cowden, with a special request for the Hebrew's Chorus from Nabucco. Friends from the London Philharmonic, including David Temple, came and sang and this led to other ad hoc choirs. Later through our friend, Tricia Denning, we sang annually in Tunbridge Wells shopping precinct in aid of Hospice in the Weald. The singers were of excellent standard and provided a rich source of singers for weddings, funeral etc., for which we were asked to arrange choirs. I was asked by Tricia 'to wave a finger' at carol singing and so my conducting continued well into the millennium.

It was during these years that we sang carols around the houses wi8thy some chosen friends. One of the houses was that of Jean Rook , the notorious Fleet Street columnist and her husband. On one occasion we arrived when she was having a party, and after the first carol which we sang in the hall, a Welsh voice was heard to say "That was very good". To my horror it was Sir Geraint Evans the well known baritone. I immediately offered him the baton but he said "You carry on maestro and I will join the basses" so I had the privilege of having to conduct one who had sung with leading conductors all over the world. One does find oneself in unplanned situations. Another was when I had to answer for the choir to Andre Previn during a recording and persuaded him to come and engage with us and explain what he required, which seemed to work and I was invited by him to listen to the playbacks with the engineers.

I don't have a favourite composer or list of desert island discs. I like them all at different times. I can get absorbed in Anglican liturgical music because it is ingrained; Handel or Mozart opera or Schubert or Bach piano music please equally. There is always more to discover and while I still have hearing and can distinguish beauty from noise, and sound from amplification, I will continue to listen as the moderns make records of the old and explore sounds on their own. I can listen with concentration to new music but I can't listen to jazz for long. I enjoy swing, musicals and cabaret. While at Cambridge I was smitten with the footlights music of Julian Slade and others and would sit at the piano and improvise my own tunes in similar style, dominant sevenths etc. It was all bit "Want of girl" music as Alistair Cooke once called it, as it had been in the time of Noel Coward and Ivor Novello. Edward has a liking for improvising in the style of Oscar Peterson which I admire.

From time to time Suzanne and I ventured into organising concerts as at Edenbridge, using both Hever and Penshurst Place. These were for The Friends of St John Charity and we were fortunate to find a ready supply of artists, such as Emma Johnson, Anne Sophie van Otter, early in their careers, the wind section from the LPO and Richard Stillgoe. On these occasions I wrote programme notes, as Tony had done. I still like to read books about music. Dear John Alldis once said that I had a feel for music like a professional, which pleased me. When leaving the Council of the London Philharmonic Orchestra, David Marcou, the then chairman, wrote to me saying that I "brought to the discussion an obvious affection for the orchestra resulting from years of performing with the band."

When Tony died in 1983, the battle Festival which had been a continuing interest of his suggested that there should be a commission in his memory. The family was asked to agree and in conjunction with South East Arts Michael Berkekey composed a clarinet quintet. This was performed at the festival later that year by Andrew Mariner and is now in the repertoire and published. There was a great turnout from the family who had subscribed Tony had been at Oxford with Michael's father Lennox and that Neville Mariner had worked with him on devising programmes for the Festival. It was a privilege to be involved in this

We were fortunate to work as ushers at Glyndebourne for twelve (Suzanne did fourteen) years after retirement. This enabled me to learn and study opera in performance, thumb through scores, and play them on the piano. It was good to see the professionalism around us and eavesdrop on them even if it was only gossip. It helped me understand theatre lighting and design, now that Juliet is in the profession. I like to think that I can still make passable sound while singing in Holy Trinity, our church at Coleman's Hatch and I enjoy madrigal singing at Tallow Chandlers' Hall in the City where we meet for dinner and sing monthly in the winter. Old friends such as Chris Munday ask us to sing in choirs, but the effort is becoming greater each time although certain music tempts me; perhaps not Gerontius but Mozart and Brahms Requiem, or Elijah and the Creation yes. I can still wander to a piano and play through songs and scores a get pleasure from mastering something from my repertoire. As the Schumann song goes "Ich kann wohl manchmal singen" which means yes I can sing sometimes if sadly! Through

Chris we met Derek Dowsett, a tenor, who came to sing, and stayed to play cricket with the Laodiceans. I also play piano duets with Charles when he comes for the weekend.

The Purcell song "Music for a while, shall all my cares beguile" is a part of my life. Recreation or re-creation? More than that, because performance gives one confidence and rehearsal is training in accuracy and presentation. William Byrd said "Since singing is a glorious thing, I wish all men would learn to sing." I often think what a better place the world would be if this were true. Watching Gareth Malone on television makes me realise that others think the same. Coming from a musical family, I can look back on many occasions, and have photographs to remind me. Continuing to practice is important to me. I get great pleasure from seeing my grandchildren performing and enjoying it as I did. Nick and Edward at John's and the girls at music competitions in Mansfield. When I look back on these occasions, the nervousness, the anticipation, and above all the sheer joy of participating, when each human being reaches something beyond self and is striving for the unattainable. To describe this experience is impossible, but I have recordings which are a reminder of those occasions and their importance in my life.

Perhaps I can continue to sing and play for many further years and enjoy the music which has been part of my life, provided nobody is listening.

CHAPTER 11

"That good thing that was committed unto thee, keep by the Holy Ghost which dwelleth in us"
1 Timothy 1 v 14

From an early age I was used to clergy visiting the home. At Ardeevin, Padre Halahan, the chaplain from the war was a regular visitor and I believe that he played a part in my first birthday party and I was baptised by him. I use the expression clergy rather than priest, probably because of my Ulster Protestant upbringing, which avoided expressions which, although Anglican, could be interpreted as Catholic. Sunday services and a visit from the incumbent were part of our lives in Helens Bay, and we were often visited by the eccentric pipe smoking Canon Capsey. Clergy and the Sunday observance were never an infringement on our lives.

From an early age my diaries show that I recorded something of the sermon, what the preacher was like, and how the music was performed. To this day certain Sundays are good and some not so good. At St George's we had worship at the start of each day, run by the pupils. It therefore seemed quite natural for me to be confirmed at the age of thirteen, at St George's. The middle of the road Canon, Stafford Crawley, prepared us. I have his notes to this day where he explained consubstantiation, transubstantiation, and gave us books to read such as The World Christ Knew and Christian Outlines, and inculcated that habit of finding a book to read each Lent.

I was confirmed by Archbishop Cosmo Gordon Lang, retired and therefore available for duty at the Royal Peculiar in St George's Chapel, with the singing of Attwood's "Come Holy Ghost." The same anthem was sung at the Confirmation of the then Princes Elizabeth in the private chapel at the Castle, another occasion in which we participated.

It was perhaps the text which he gave us from Timothy "That good thing that was committed to you" which remained fixed in my mind and has stayed with me.

Regular worship on Sundays was the pattern of my life. Sometimes I went twice a day joining the Presbyterians in the evening to see what they were up to. In the days before television and with Sabbath observance preventing sport, church attendance was both a form of fellowship and mental stimulus. What did you think of the sermon was a question at Sunday lunch. When Uncle Jack Shillington was there, it was a regular topic. When an unfortunate cleric quoted Kipling "You are nearer God's heart in a garden than anywhere else on earth" he accused him of trying to empty the church.[3]

Mo still retained her Methodist_roots. She introduced me to the preaching of Dr Leslie Weatherhead, a Methodist preacher of his day, when in Belfast, and in London I would get my mental stimulus from him, and my spiritual from the Cathedrals or All Saints, Margaret Street. At Cambridge I heard the American evangelist Billy Graham, and the quietly spoken Cyril Garbett, Archbishop of York. At that age I was immature enough to think that Graham had the edge, but never followed it up. I was very much a worshipper at the chapel at King's.

During the 1960s in Mansfield, Arthur Wilson asked me to fill in during the interregnum with a series of worship which he did at the hospital. Just give them something like a parable, and avoid personal hymns like Abide with Me. The young of the parish would organise it. All I had to do was turn up, take them in my car, say the prayers and preach. Arthur also introduced us to hosting a house group and invited me to take part in quizzes.

The three outstanding priests in my life have David Bartleet, Richard Mason and Paddy Craig. Each in their time gave me something at the latter part of the twentieth century which set me up for the new millennium. David welcomed us into the Church at Edenbridge, at a time when we both felt we needed to be reconciled with the Church and he was able to arrange this for us with David Say, Bishop of Rochester. He was an enlightened and thoughtful priest. We continued to meet after he had moved away to be first Rector of Bromley and then Bishop of Tonbridge. Soon after our arrival, we took part in Benjamin Britten's "Noyes Fludde" in Edenbridge Church. I understudied the Voice of God. We had much to talk about and he became a member of the small madrigal group we set up in our house. His successor, Richard Mason, inherited us and we both to became chairman of two of his special committees. We had the benefit of his pastoral care and encouragement at a time when he had problems in his own life. He taught me about bereavement and how to talk to people, a facility at which he was very accomplished, as exemplified in his contact with John Osborne, the playwright.[4] It was in Edenbridge that I had my first experience of Parish Church Councils and working with community groups such as Friends of St John . We made many friends through this.

After we moved to Cowden, we found our way to Coleman's Hatch where Paddy Craig, a fellow Ulsterman, was the Rector. He turned up one day to ask me to take a service in his place. He coached me well and this led to me thinking that Ii might have a part to play in my retirement in some kind of lay ministry. Paddy challenged me and I met him. This all started in 1994. The ordinand team in the diocese met me and we agreed a programme of study, and after about two years I was admitted as a lay assistant at Holy Trinity, Coleman's Hatch, a duty which I have continued to fulfil. Paddy encouraged vibrant worship, no frills and broad church. He avoided his fellow priests and stuck to his own rules. He was a great pastoral visitor of Church of Ireland training. He taught me to be uninhibited and to enjoy leading a service in the way that Doc H had taught us, that is to put everything that we had into singing. After Paddy retired I was able, with Nicholas Leviseur, then recently ordained as curate, to run the interregnum for about a year and to become stand in deacon in the parish. It was not possible to proceed to be ordained, but it was not from want of encouragement and recommendation from clergy friends and supporters. I did investigate a theology degree but was too elderly to do it. Writing in 2009, after a year of illness of the present incumbent, I can truthfully say that I have had to take services and preach without prior notice, lead funerals, and administer the (reserved) sacrament both to the housebound and from the altar.

Although the role of clergy has changed in my lifetime and all is not as it was, there is still a feeling for the Church of England as I knew it from the beginning. I confess that I have always been moved in a personal way by performances of St Mathew Passion, St John and the Dream of Gerontius and have found both grief and sublime joy in music, as the ultimate understanding of what our earthly experience can be. To take part in these works has also been an experience, although I had to keep remembering that it was technique and skill which made the performance. Guilini made a preconcert speech to us once about the word "amateur" meaning it was your love which sustained the performance and gave it something extra. He had a point. It was when I gave up being in the choir that I thought I should try and communicate something to others about what this music had meant to me.

It must have been in the teens that I began to be interested in visiting churches, a hobby which I shared with Miles. I remember when he was on leave from the army we went on a cathedral hopping tour, taking in Ely, Peterborough and York. It was on an expedition to York Minster with a friend from Trent that I became interested in cathedral architecture and and the different periods of carvings and glass. They had a guide there of eloquence and imagination. Objects such as the Dean's eye window at York or the Angel choir at Lincoln stood out. This interest was without doubt stimulated by John Saltmarsh of Kings who took delight in showing us what to look out for in the chapel, so that I was able to entertain my guests with my own observations.

My children used to complain when on holiday that I would wander off to look at a parish church and leave them in the car. Having attended lectures in Cambridge by Nicholas Pevsner, his writings, and those of John Betjeman, have always been a *vade mecum* as they must have been to many in my generation, in stirring interest. It was an interest in local history which attracted me, and finding amusing effigies or memorials such as that of a choir member at Norwich Cathedral. Certain priests of the present era rather scorn this veneration as a substitute for faith, but to me there is something about a place where as T.S Eliot says "prayer has been valid", and generations of people have worshipped. Visiting the Romney Marsh churches with their stories of the plague, penance and other acts of faith, only underscore my own faith and give me a close link to that eternity, in which I believe. Strangely enough it was a young Israeli whom I met in Tel Aviv who surprisingly said to me how much he liked the English Parish Church and its atmosphere of tranquillity and peace.

I have a lifelong friend, Michael Rees, from age eleven at St George's. He has continued as a good friend exchanging letters and cards through our lives. Not a chorister as was his brother the Radiologist, Simon, he converted to Catholicism, while at Cambridge, a process which I recall discussing with him along the backs, and in retirement became a monk with the community on Caldey Island off Tenby. I enjoyed his company on a visit there in 2006, a year after he had taken his vows. The studied faith of the fifteen brethren, their regular offices, devout and yet learned men who were at peace with the world and mixed with tourists and visitors quite sensibly and amicably. They made me welcome and had time for others. As we walked up to the headland recalling our lives, the pain of others and the beauty of the headland, we recaptured something of the glory of God in his creation and how those who lived distant from the mainland could contemplate something of our purpose and our fallibility while being fixed on the eternity for which we all strive. I have always found beauty in holiness. Suzanne remembers the day when we heard that her mother had died and we were in France and I suggested that we visited Chartres and just sat there for a few moments. I have found my way to churches when Ruth or a member of the family was having an operation and I needed to pray for them at that time.

In the seventies we became friendly with Colin and Betty Busby. Colin played the trombone in the London Philharmonic Orchestra, and was a talented photographer. We used to visit their home in Ashleigh Gardens. Betty, a pharmacist, developed cancer but instead of it curtailing her life she became proactive with others who suffered and her faith became stronger. She insisted on taking communion at least twice a week and in her remarkable book[5] she writes of the importance of that prayer of humble access which begins the service. She lived for several years after the professionals had given her up and amusingly said that various clergy claimed the credit for her survival.

While at a conference in Rome, I was entertained by my friends the Valoris, Duccio told me to concentrate on one period if I were to go sightseeing. After a tour of the villa Borghese, I managed a good number of Bernini churches before the sun set and just got to St John Lateran to hear a German choir in familiar Bach chorales. Suzanne and I have enjoyed many occasions the Valoris both in England and Italy. They provide us with a source of opportunities . We borrowed their apartment in a condominium Santa Severa for a late October holiday in 1978, the year of the two Popes. I happened to be in Jerusalem when Pius died and we arrived at the Vatican the morning after John Paul I had died, but we carried out our visit to the Sistine Chapel, and apartment nonetheless. The Valori family now have houses in Bomarzo in Tuscany, which we have visited and the next generation of both our families have got to know each other.

When I was president of the Nottingham Chamber of Commerce in 1967, one of my officers was a Moral Rearmament enthusiast, and invited Conrad Hunte, the West Indian cricketer to speak at a meeting. He was a sportsman I admired, and when I happened to refer to the lack of responsibility of the press, he kept me in mind and sent me a copy of Peter Howard's book with a covering letter. The follow up was an invitation to an evening in a drawing room in Belgravia, not far from the Westminster Theatre, where I met some well to do members of MRA. After the ladies had served us with a tea and eats, they withdrew and there started a group disclosure about why each one had turned to MR as their rule of living. Confessions abounded about cheating employers, being successful without caring for the consequence, doing without God, who was unnecessary, all in turn and the leader turned to me. I knew it was coming, and was desperately trying to think of something awful in my life to relate, but all I did was to relate that I was a practising Christian and had tried to lead my life in the way I believed I should, and that I would continue trying to do so. Keep that which is committed to you. So after a polite thank you I departed. I continued to receive newsletters. I used the restaurant at the Westminster Theatre, I lost touch with MR, although I was aware of the efforts being made by Conrad Hunte, both on and off the field, which subsequently appeared in his obituary in Wisden[6]

In this rather varied panoply what do I believe and take away? My faith and worship have become a part of life which I would find difficult to do without. I enjoy and continue to read theology and various writings on the subject. I believe faith is an intellectual discipline, as it has been handed down to us from Augustine and Aquinas, to mention but two. In my own time Michael Ramsey and fellow Ulsterman C.S. Lewis have been great influences. At times when I see what a parish priest has to do, I wonder if he only needs to be pastoral, and whether too much theology from the pulpit is right for a congregation. What is known as dumbing down I canot stand, particularly the self gratification which comes with it. It is neither good theatre, worship in the beauty of holiness, nor to the greater glory of God. We do need to remember the mystery of the Creator. Too much propaganda, as the philosopher Donald MacKinnon says, defeats philosophical exposition. I cannot but accept what Peter Mullen, chaplain to our livery company, preaches and proclaims in the press and from the pulpit of St Michael's Cornhill. I did try to modernise and enjoyed some of the prayers the new liturgy of the 1960s Series 1,2and 3, and although they have now disappeared, I still have the prayers with me.

I have frequently been exasperated with the Church of England, and understand the frustration which others feel, but in the end it seems to muddle through and my hope is that someday someone will arrive and with charisma, who is able to see and make us understand the mysteries that have been committed to us and so fill the spiritual vacuum, which exists in our material and secular society, built on celebrity and success culture. There are some out there at present, whom I admire and support and I hope that their ministries will succeed.

It's easy to condemn, and crabbed age makes one critical, but at 79 I am still exploring what it is that the Creator has to offer us in Prayer, reading and worship. With church friends, we meet weekly at "Time Out" and we have no inhibitions as we meditate and seek to find God in our daily lives, in a less structured but thoughtful way. My spiritual director is a theologian at St Barnabas College, Lingfield, Ivan Clutterbuck, "a Pelican in the Wilderness,"[7] as he calls himself, but one who continues at 94 to look for hope, and finds fresh inspiration from teaching scripture based on the gospels, for which he has been much acclaimed. He and I continue to hope and Peter Mullen's idea that being born again as not a once for all experience but a continual revelation throughout life makes much sense. As Charles Wesley put it in his hymn "Still let me guard the Holy Fire, and still stir up the gift in me"

---

[3] For Jack Shillington's attitude to army chaplains "Lion Rampant" by Wollacombe. He is the fictional Ben, a good characterisation as those who knew him will vouch [4]John Osborne by John Heilpern p402 [5]The Rice has Boiled by Chen Yu   [6]Wisden   [7] "Pelican in the Wilderness" by Ivan Clutterbuck

CHAPTER 12

My family and others

This is a difficult part to write, as I must cover the breakdown of the family and why. It is also about growing up and all that. Both male and female write about conquests, even disappointments, kiss and tell, but that is not my style. We are put on this earth as male and female and we rub along together. Whether we ever understand each other I don't know but it is a constant pursuit. Happiness is an overused word which we unfortunately pick up from romantic tales. Compatibility is a better one and partnership better than that. In exploring it all during the latter half of the twentieth century many of us made mistakes which perhaps this present generation in the new millennium can avoid.

I'm not sure when I started to harbour romantic ideas about the opposite sex. Sidney and I had no romantic attachment but we had our birthday parties at the same time and remained friends until she died in 2003. She was very much the sister of my own age which I never had, and we were in touch at various stages of our lives and her husband Michael has become a close friend. We were very much together when we played tennis at Craigavad and between us we organised a mixed party of acceptable people in our teens. Then there were the private dances, a feature of Ulster life, mainly in houses when we dance to Pride of Erin Waltz and looked at the flickering lights across the Belfast Lough. They were a part of the Christmas holidays. At school it was always good to tell the chaps about a girl one had met, to produce a photograph, write and receive letters.

Cambridge I have described elsewhere but during the three years my affections changed so that by the end I was in a state of confusion and embarrassment but that must have been a regular state of affairs for those of us who came from single sex schools. We never thought about forming relationships or going on holiday together, as became the norm later. There were a few who saw each other daily and walked hand in hand but I was not one of them.

I met Ruth Baldwin at the end of 1952. Our parents had been friends and colleagues in Nigeria, and I was invited to stay with them while looking for a career. I was not the only one on the premises in this position so it was quite by chance that we got together. I admired her enthusiasm for her teaching, her self confidence, which was much in excess of that of her elder sister Rachel, so with similar family backgrounds and being of the same age it was perhaps natural for us to get together. Engagement and marriage followed at a very young age for us both, but there were complications about where we should live; she had a good job, and my location in Ulster with the family business was meant to be only temporary, but when the job came to an end, I was back where I started after Cambridge with a wife and very soon a child on the way.

Looking back we probably suffered from not having a place where we could settle down. Silsoe provided the centre for our lives as the family grew. We did have a small flat in the grounds of Newstead Abbey for a few months after Nicholas was born and he was christened in the local church, so we had hoped to settle there when I became established. As it turned out we missed that stage until some five years later, when, with a larger family, we bought our first house in Mansfield, a sizable property which became our family home, if beyond our means at that time. By this time the Baldwin family had moved to Hardwick near Cambridge and when Nicholas went to St John's Cambridge became a magnet. It was not easy for me to go there regularly and during my time as president of Junior Chamber of Commerce and also due to pressure of my work, I was spending large times on my own in Mansfield, while my family were at Hardwick .

Suzanne and I met though singing and we both found that we were not really happy with our circumstances and gradually came together and fell in love. When we made the break I was already taking tranquilisers and promoted to a job in London at Hobart House on an increased salary. As the divorce went through, we moved and found ourselves in Edenbridge, where, thanks to the church community and Rev David Bartleet, we were able to make a fresh start and, in the words of St Paul in the Philippians, "press on" and we both kept ourselves busy building a new life together and remembering to look forward rather than backwards.

I failed Ruth and my children but I have tried to make it up and my children are a very important part of my life as my character and aspirations have developed. My parents, siblings and cousins have been a great support to both of us in making it work and I am very fond of my extended family. Suzanne's family have been a rock of strength and both in laws lived long enough to be good companions, as are her sisters Pamela and Jane and her brother Robin, with whom I sang in the choir, his wife Clare, family and love of music and we are surrounded by many memories and enthusiasms from our own lives together and the friends in common that we have picked up on the way.

There have been wayward moments, as in most cases and for this I make no cover up but there are always two people and two families to consider. As I have said elsewhere passion is not enough; common interests and pursuits can last for a time, but partnership is what really counts and I have seen this in Edward and Marianne , and in Juliet and Michael. Suzanne and I have found it in, in our project at Gigouzac, our house in France and in our joint working as volunteers for BESO. Others have noticed it and remarked on it, and we have done our bit with others when required. It was in Nepal, when she had to go home early and I was left behind, that for the first time I felt that I had been deprived of a limb and realised that as someone once said, we were really joined at the hip.

Mabel had two special friends, Val Tennant and Eileen Cowdy. Two more different people you could not find. Val had been at Headington, and came from a well connected Birmingham family, the Nettlefolds and her mother was a Chamberlain. She had extreme left wing leanings in her single days. She married Peter Tennant, from a well-known Scottish family and who worked in a Quaker medical unit during the war. They both went on to work at Corymeela, well known for spiritual reconciliation. Eileen came from the Cowdy clan who used to holiday in Newcastle with the Shillingtons. The Cowdy sisters were younger than Mabel, but lively and what Mabel would have called "hard hitting girls", always rushing around and jumping off diving boards which as a child I found very frightening. When I met them later in the seventies they were all inclusive, Irish welcoming, still laughing and talking loudly although delicate in health. They had all done service in the war. Eileen was unmarried and so was a friend to many married women as a shoulder on which to lean and a confidante to many people. She also picked up the siblings, an honorary godparent as it was always meant to be. She was argumentative in all things, devout and a regular church goer and pillar. When she and her mother retired to Bladon near Oxford, she was a village person, local counsellor and equally distributed of loving kindness to all around her.

Mabel retained her Irishness despite twenty years in Battle where she entered into the spirit of everything which Tony had wanted on retirement, music, church and their garden which he was able to enjoy up to his death in 1983. She had her Ulster dialect phrases such a tatie, shuggledy, toti wee to mention only a handful. When she couldn't remember a name it was "who d'ye call it" and "not in our ken." She finally did some teaching at the local secondary school, and the house saw two family weddings in 1963 and 1973 in St Mary's and their golden wedding in August 1989, which was a double event for family and another for the retired colonials from Nigeria who seemed to be resident in Sussex. Tony was much involved with the Battle Art festival, and the choral society. He got Neville Mariner interested and whenever the national anthem was required Tony would play the grand piano.

His playing the piano, he was an accomplished singer of light music to entertain guests at Glenmachan and elsewhere, and reading aloud to us are the memories of him which I have in my childhood, as he was absent for long periods before and during the war. In his retirement we got to know each other and his letters to me contain his profound thoughts. His amusing turn of phrase was characteristic as many of his friends recalled. One of memory was at the choir school in Dean's yard, Westminster when he was visiting Miles. The ecclesiastical architecture of the hall where they dined contained a number of statues at one end. At this time Field marshal Montgomery (Monty) used to visit the school and had given them a photograph, Tony glanced at this photograph, hung among the statues of the saints and exclaimed "Thou madest him a little lower than the angels" (Psalm 8)

It was in 1950, my first long vac when, as I had succumbed to illness again, I was given the opportunity to visit them in Kaduna Northern Nigeria. My recollections of all of this are in an essay which I wrote for John Saltmarsh when I returned to Kings, on how I saw life in the country and the functioning of native and colonial administration. It was also my first chance of seeing a father go to work, come back and hear about what he was doing. During those eight weeks I was able to enjoy the environment of living in the tropics and the appropriate life for a person of my age. In Kaduna we had a garden with canna lilies and an avocado tree (I had not come across avocados previously), grapefruits on trees and the southern hemisphere stars at night. I often wonder what happened to the gardens which the colonial servants created and cherished during the Empire. Somebody said that the greatest contribution of the west to the east is the cataloguing and analysing of fauna and flora which remain a perpetual record. It was a perfect way to spend a long vac, as I had my own wing of the house and balcony for reading and playing my clarinet, my personal servant Shehu, the junior to Ali my father's trusted steward, who woke me in the morning, prepared my clothes and was on hand to minister to my wants, depending on how much Hausa I could muster. I learnt to drive the car, and there was tennis at the club with Joan Foster, later Russell, who still resides in Lewes Sussex, and parties with Brenda Stapleton, now in her nineties and who lives in the next village. After Dinner at Government House, the men were invited by the host to "visit Africa" in his garden. We formed pecking order according to rank, I being at the rear with the ADC as we relieved ourselves among the plants the fruits of his hospitality. While on tour with Dennis Hibbert , we were stranded on the road and ignored by missionaries who, as it were, passed by on the other side. I went to see tin mines in Jos, stayed at Pop Bowler's rest house, and finished at Bauchi where the emir showed me his harem. We met there one who was to be the great statesman of Nigeria, Abubakar Tafawa Balewa to whose charity I subscribe to this day. As recorded by Trevor Clark, his biographer, I was present at an important historical occasion in July 1950 at the House of Assembly, [8] and, sitting in Strangers' Gallery, was impressed by his speech proposing the modernisation and reform of the system of native administration. This was carefully crafted, with quotations from Goldsmith and Lord Lugard, whose policy of indirect rule had been the bulwark of Nigerian government. I became familiar with some of the amusing Hausa riddles, and the only blot on the experience was a riding accident, which I broke an arm, when my runaway horse collided with a motor cyclist who sadly later died of gangrene and I had to attend the inquest.

I have much admiration for Tony's colleagues whom I have met over the years for their loyalty and resourcefulness at a time when politicians didn't really value this during the dismemberment of empire. A publication the history of schools 1959 in Hausa and English records "as late as the nineteen twenties young Mr. Shillingford, Junior superintendent, set off for Maiduguri on horseback with a caravan of a hundred bearers and twenty seven camels." Rory Stewart has so aptly put it in "Occupational Hazards" (Picador 2006) "colonial officers served for forty years, spoke the local languages fluently, and risked their lives and health, administering justice and collecting revenue in tiny, isolated districts, protected only by a small local levy. They often ruled indirectly, " advising" local kings, tolerating the flaws in their administration and toppling them only if they seriously endangered the security of the state. They put strong emphasis on local knowledge, courage, initiative and probity, but they were ruthless in controlling dissent and wary of political change". They organised local schools and hospitals and achieved results with improvements in educating women in traditional Muslim cultures. How different it is today when everyone is on short time contracts with little time to make their mark .

My parents' generation have subsequently been much criticised for colonialism. At the break up of the Empire, Tony and Mabel had reached the end of their careers. The younger people were less fortunate and had to find other work in mid life. One of their friends presented them with a book in which he had inscribed this extract from an article "faces of Empire on which the sun should not set" by Douglas Brown in the Sunday telegraph 5/10/75 "But it is not primarily to the politicians nor the technologists who have changed the face of Asia and Africa, that my mind goes gratefully back as the colonial chapter closes. I think rather of the countless men and women who in missionary compounds, jungle clinics, district commissioners' bungalows and every kind of harsh environments strove tirelessly, and without personal ambition, for the good of their fellow human beings as they saw it. They laboured in their day and generation, often within a limited appreciation of what the ultimate harvest was likely to be , but it is largely because of them that I do not feel abashed when youngsters sing "Land of Hope and Glory" on the last Night of the Proms."

Miles and I were close as brothers and it was a great sadness when he died in 2006 before he reached 70. Despite the distance between us in age, we had much in common and we enjoyed many things together. We were both choristers and my early diaries show that I was protective of him during his growing up when he missed Mabel greatly while she was in Nigeria. He wrote to me when in America and in the army, and his letters are a commentary on how he found things there particularly the difference in law. We were close, although different in temperament and our last time together was in Youghall near Cork for our nephew Tom Fletcher's wedding to Louise Fitzgerald. It was tragic that I joined the guard of honour for Tom as an honorary member of his cricket club, only later that year to hold an oar as Miles body was taken from his home in Suffolk by the undertakers. Perhaps my strongest memories are of him in chambers in New Square, which he occupied throughout his legal career, and on his boat, hand on tiller looking into the mainsail . He continued to live in the same house in Albert Bridge Road, a magnet for the family and where he and Judi, whom he married in 1963, when he was teaching at Michigan University brought up their family of three girls, Tanya, Stephanie and Katie.

Paula was a year older than Miles, and different from us in being a mathematician and logical thinker. She was the practical one they all said, and her feminine character quickly established itself in the family, her organisational ability, and her forgetfulness which people found a disarming charm, and her lengthy telephone conversations. She married Rhoderic Pentycross and they spent all their lives in Cheltenham where he taught at Dean Close. Illness again took its toll and she died before she was able to relax in retirement, but she was highly regarded by both pupils and others with whom she came in contact as her friend Sue Page made clear at her memorial service. Her three children are scattered, with Louise in Greece, Hilary at home and Graham my godson bringing up his family in South London. Her involvement with Brownies goes back to the Shillingtons of the Portadown Sunday school.

Deborah was born in 1948, rather a surprise, but strange to relate Suzanne's sister Jane was also a late addition to her family. Being brought up in the days when nannies had gone and travelling was easier, unlike us she was with Mabel and Tony for most of her childhood in either country. She and I as sole survivors remain close despite the difference in age, and in generation. This is through music, church and common family interests, and similarly to Paula, she runs food stop a voluntary organisation to support the needy. Mark Fletcher her husband whom she married in 1978 is a renowned teacher of English as a foreign language, and her eldest son Tom after Oxford is now in the Foreign and Commonwealth office. Luke and Rebecca and John, who is Downs's syndrome, are the other members of this happy nuclear and very Christian family. Mabel spent her last twenty five years with Deborah at Folkestone and this kept her alive in both interest and health.

My own four children and Suzanne's three sons Simon, Charles and Adrian are part of our combined family. In their different ways they fit in to life around us and we enjoy seeing them. Simon and I are close in church matters and in reading; Nicholas and Charles are into cricket and sport. Edward has good head for business judgement and is compassionate although he hides it and I see him achieving much as has his wife Marianne who contributes her own talents. Adrian is an astute lawyer, with left leanings. Juliet's theatre achievements have given us a great kick and she and Michael are a happy combination in theatre. Their three children Daniel, Anna and Jake have been given the chance to develop their talents in different ways, sport and performing arts, as has Nicholas daughter, Nina, a keen ballerina. Felicity has persevered on her own by bringing up her daughter Eve. She has a strong character and definite ideals. There is a sense of calm about her and she and Eve are very much a team together and have survived despite everything. Added to them are Suzanne's cousin Julian Waller who made his home with us after he left school and, despite severe problems with his feet from an early age, has made much of his life. He married Julia, and we are delighted to be surrogate Grandparents to their three children Vanessa and Beth, now married, and Tim. Edward and Marianne and their children, Jack, Ella and Molly have been given every opportunity in their upbringing to travel, and widen their interests in many ways. We have enjoyed holidays with them on Strangford Lough at Castle Ward and in Venice where we had an apartment together in 2006.

Paul Hughes was a great friend during his lifetime. We met at Kings, played rugby, and became close. He was a year ahead of me, but taught the choir school so we saw him for the extra time and then when I came to Nottingham, he was established as a barrister and we saw much of him socially. Godfather and bachelor he was a confidant but we sadly fell out and it was Suzanne who visited him before he died. My first year at Kings was a happy one and I became friendly with Paul and Tony Laughton and my contemporary Christopher Hamshaw Thomas, the son of a don at Downing. Our lives were to cross continuously but it was the Oliphant Society which we started in Kings, as a refuge for wind players who could use the available music from the Rowe and Mann library to play, previously unknown and unperformed music such as the fall of Jerusalem. We kept minutes and it is recorded that we attracted interest of such musicians as Philip Radcliffe and Thurston Dart, to participate with us to blow little known or strange arrangements of popular music. It amuses me to think of this undergraduate prank all meetings being started with the ceremonial blowing of the Oliphant, an elephant horn, such as blown by Roland. Birnie Evans was another good friend, and godfather to Nicholas and Roger Gaunt who started a choir while at Kings and then a festival in Endelion, Cornwall.

Michael Rees was a friend whom I retained from St George's days. Although not a chorister he and I were close since age eleven, and remained friends at Cambridge. His career was kindled by a yearning for Catholicism, and for thirty years he wanted to join the Cistercians at Caldey Island not far from his home in Carmarthen. His wish was granted and about a year after he was admitted to the Order in 2006 I visited him and spent a memorable day attending the offices and walking with him around the island before he saw me off to the mainland port of Tenby. I long to return.

There are many others, with whom I have enjoyed friendship over the years and with whom I exchanged letters at a time when that was the main form of communication. We sustained each other and kept up a shared understanding and loyalty to each other. The circle has obviously shrunk with time and age, but there were always times when we turned up in each other's lives.

[8]*A Right Honourable Gentleman, Abubakar of the Black Rock by Trevor Clark .Edward Arnold 1991 p135*

CHAPTER 13

Play the game

I don't know who it was who first threw a ball at me. Judging by my mother's tennis ability, it may have been her. Being the first boy I was expected to excel at games, so I was probably a disappointment to her, although we did play mixed doubles in several tennis tournaments.

At St George's I just made the unbeaten football team of 1942 and became vice captain of cricket, a game which I have treasured throughout my life. At the end of the Summer term, we were allowed to watch games at Eton and my match cards from these games show that I once saw Gubby Allen of the bodyline tour, playing for the Eton Ramblers against a College team which included Peter Blake.

I remember my housemaster at Trent, Charles Lang, being surprised that I could be a good head of house without the ability to excel at games, which he thought was essential in leadership. Tennis and golf were common pastimes in the family so I was coached in both these, playing mixed tennis in the summer holidays with Sidney and others. It was all part of growing up and often one could get the better of someone older with a good shot.

As one gets older, one has to watch younger people becoming better than oneself, so disillusion sets in and with it apathy. It's like Sir Andrew Aguecheek " I was promising once ". It's all to do with what is now known as a mental attitude and practice. I've seen the same symptoms in my grandson Dan, and, to an extent Nicholas, as both of them have dropped out through injury or disappointment when they had talent beyond anything which I could offer. You can read so much about sportsmen and women now showing how they overcome handicaps and win through to greater things by mental resolution. It depends on whether you continue to play for enjoyment or give up and become a critic or a spectator.

Uncle Brewer took me to Lords in the summer of 1943, and I had seen such legends as Constantine, but It was Charles Lang, although he realised my limitations, who introduced me to the enjoyment of sport as a spectator and follower. I managed to be allowed to watch the South Africans at Trent Bridge in the summer of 1947. As I look round the ground today, I can recall where I was then when I saw the South Africans, Alan Melville and Dudley Nourse put on a record put on a record partnership of over 300 runs each scoring centuries in a total of 533. My diary entry for Saturday 7th June, which was the first day, noted that "Melville was elegant and easy, Nourse hard hitting and forceful." Norman Yardley, the England captain, came on to bowl just before lunch, as he often did. Godfrey Evans was " wizard behind the stumps" and, of course, there was Alec Bedser.

It was the beginning of a new era in my life and when I was ill the following year and missed seeing Don Bradman, I would tune in to Arlott, Macgillvray and Alston (himself an old Trident) and hear those summaries by Swanton and Robertson-Glasgow. A door opened which has never closed and which has tempt me to cricket grounds, Fenners, Lords or Trent Bridge, when I should have been somewhere else. It was only on retirement that I was able to open a bottle of wine with others before the end of mornings play and say, in all conscience, this is it; I don't have to be anywhere else. It is a great feeling. I enjoy my present memberships at Sussex and Notts, Hove and Trent Bridge are both different in character and in both places I always find someone to talk to. There are the grounds of Horsham, Arundel and Tunbridge Wells to add to my list of my favourite grounds.

Being housebound and ill in the summer of 1948, I became an addicted listener to what was to become Test Match Special. That was the summer of Bradman's last tour. At the same time Miles and James Douglas were becoming interested in the stars of the game, so that when we all went on holiday to Rostrevor, I found I had cricketing companions. Although encased head and shoulders in plaster of Paris, I did manage to play garden cricket, and James recalls my sweeping shots and those of Paula, both there and in the garden at Holly House. He remains a cricketing companion and as he was then and a mine of cricketing knowledge. My nephews Tom and Luke Fletcher were both garden cricketers at Folkestone and continue to play in the Strollers, a team they set up and I have the cap in recognition of setting up their first match at Cowden in the early years of the millennium.

I managed to play in my age group at Rugby football right through my schooldays, so it was a disappointment to miss my final term when, as a second fifteen colour of the previous year, I might have made the fifteen. Coming to King's I was determined to start again and turned up on Scholars Piece as a freshman to meet Paul Hughes, Martin Scott, Gerald Smart and Tony Laughton, seniors in the club and we trained together. Other freshmen, Gerry Taylor and (Prof) Roy Willis became part of the college squad and were encouraged by Tom Wells, a New Zealand graduate, who went on to play for the University and to get two England trials as full back. Tom put us through our paces. Each Saturday there was a match at Grange Road when the University side played the English and Welsh club sides in turn. This was the build up to Twickenham and winning a blue, so reputations rose and fell on those occasions. We had international half backs from Wales and Scotland who were to face each other in the internationals in the New Year and an England wing, a Welsh forward and Scottish centre. In the summer term there was cricket at Fenners, and I came up with both David Sheppard and Peter May, who were to captain England and were the last generation of amateurs. There were others, such as Hubert Doggart and John Waite, both at King's, who distinguished themselves as first class cricketers, and with whom we rubbed shoulders in the dining hall. Visitors at Fenners were the West Indies during 1950, and various county sides, so the ex schoolboy couldn't resist the trip to the ground when he was meant to be working for his exams! Others at this time were Robin Marlar and the laconic John Warr, who features in one of my best cricket stories. Fenners is adjacent to Parkers Piece, where on Saturday the youth of Cambridge turned out to play cricket. Cambridge was down to the tail and Hubert Doggart was trying to keep the score going with Warr. Doggart was a loud caller and between the overs Warr is reputed to have said, "Can't you keep your voice down Hubert; you have already run out two people on Parkers Piece this afternoon!" I believe that is a true story.

There was plenty to talk about and sports gossip became part of life and a great bond. This has persisted and even today the drama of sport where we do not know a result until it happens and reputations are made and lost, still keep me going and is a favourite topic of conversation.

I did make the team for King's both in the first fifteen and the second. David Whitby, a friend form St George's, was also in the side. He and I had been in the historic unbeaten football side of 1942. I remember away matches at New College and Eton, and an extraordinary game of Soccer at Queen Mary College in London. In the summer we had a rugby boat and rowed in the bottom division in the May Races, keeping our bonding going. As usual I was up for anything and enjoyed life to the full. I played scrum half and coxed the boat and, although light by rugby standards, I was the heaviest Cox on the river.

It was at Broadway Damask at the time of the Coronation when a game of football was organised between the Factory and the Warehouse. I volunteered to play and of course as "gaffer's lad "was a target. After the first few minutes, playing at my usual place of inside forward, I found the ball at my left foot a few yards from the goal mouth and it went in, to great cheers from the touchline. That was too much for the goalkeeper who was a tough Belfast lad who worked in the dye house, putting yarn through dye bath. Next time in the goal mouth his fist met my nose and I was taken off, to the wailing of young girls who rushed to comfort me on the touchline as I regained composure. I can't recall much else of the game but it shows that sometimes luck is on your side and you can be in the right place at the right time when it counts.

I kept up squash, tennis, golf and even the odd game of cricket when it arrived. We played the college servants in the long vac, and I remember playing in Nigeria. Tennis was always a family game and I had played in tournaments with my mother we both went on to play with my children, particularly Nick, when he was old enough for either golf or tennis.

Years later when I was chairman of the London Philharmonic choir, I thought that relations with the orchestra could be improved if we met together on the sports field. They already boasted a football side, so I discussed with Stephen Crabtree, a bass player, who was then chairman, how we might arrange a game of cricket. For this David Ellen, a keen Kent man and player of amateur cricket, seemed the likeliest person to run it. The question was where, so with my friend John Rhodes, with whom I travelled up to London daily, we negotiated a game at Hartfield in East Sussex, where a joint team of Players and Singers from the LPO took on their second eleven in 1983. This led to many lasting friendships and continuing contests, a source of enjoyment to all concerned. As there were a number of regular cricketers in the choir, I had excluded myself and would be a bystander and facilitator of the match, but as luck would have it we were short on the day so I donned my white flannels and old studded cricket boots. I achieved something because David said that I would be in any future contests, so I found myself enjoying games of cricket and the whole business of the game for the next twenty years and still enjoy a Presidential role. The Laodiceans continue to play against Hartfield where John Rhodes, a churchman and village man of stature was a friend both on and off the field until his sudden death in 2007, and is one whose personality I admire and miss. He has been honoured in the village by an inscription and on the pavilion

The Laodiceans a name which we called our team, was the successor to this and really run by Simon and Charles but which led to inviting many of my friends, colleagues and people just picked up to play at Cowden and even tour South West France. How that came about was sheer coincidence. I heard that a team had been in Eymet, a bastide where the local English population had taken over the Stade for cricket in the summer. There was also a team at Perigeux. It was in 1992 that we ventured forth with a number of players and so began a series which was to continue for the next fifteen years. It was that year we met Jean Claude Rieudebat, a teacher of English at Aiguillon, whose stay in Somerset had given him a love for the game. He read in the local newspaper of our proposed demonstration game of cricket at Monflanquin. He threw his equipment in the boot of his car and came to join us on spec. This encounter led to regular matches at Damazan, where he persuaded the local mayor to let him have a ground set aside for cricket so that they didn't have to use the Stade and its rough rugby pitch .Our tours became the subject of a BBC broadcast on Five Life and I wrote to the Daily Telegraph about how Jean Claude and his colleagues had "managed to conjure the essence of each term" when they translated the laws into French. The word Baionnette for Yorker as both York and Bayonne were walled cities, were famous for hams, so could be associated in name with attacking weapons!

The stories of all this are legion and it was sad to have to give it up in 2007. By then I was suffering from arthritis in the knee and this was an excuse to get a Sky dish installed, which enables me to watch overseas cricket, rugby and anything which I fancy at any time in the year. It means that I have constant drama, comment discussions, and a chance to shout or acclaim without moving from my chair. It was something which I put off for a time but now I have no compunction about it. Nicholas when home from Japan loves to join us for a game, as does James Douglas from Belfast. We still have the annual match at Cowden and Nick and I usually mange a day of cricket watching at some ground, as I also do with Simon and Charlie.

A postscript must be the Indian and Bangladesh interlude. On my first Saturday in Dhaka I managed to find a game of cricket to watch at down town Dalmoondhi. Turning up as the only ex pat caused a sensation and I soon found myself watching in the pavilion sitting next to the incoming batsman, an Indian who hoped to get a summer job in English league cricket. My leisure time was made and there was no difficulty in getting pavilion seats at the many cricket occasions, being seated in comfortable chairs and brought cups of sweet tea, while the general public let off thunder flashes and got excited as they do on the subcontinent. At Guwahati it was much the same, as we arrived when the two touring sides Australia and South Africa were playing their one day game and were to stay in our hotel. That day was memorable. We were invited by Mr Das and his extended family to join them. Watching cricket there gave us a special feel of camaraderie. I umpired a game between my two client hospitals; I had to present man of the match awards which were duly reported in the state press. I was referred to as a former cricketer and Umpire from Kent! Once the secret that I loved the game was out, there was no stopping. In Calcutta it was the same; I ended up being a commentator on the public address in a Rotary match and Suzanne and I presented the trophy. This extraordinary subcontinent has such friendly and happy people that I am proud to list Gagan and Sawan Singh,who played for Damazan, and the two brothers Prakash and Bharat Rugahni and Rikki now playing for the Laodiceans. The Rhugani brothers look after my eyes in Harley Street.

It was at Cambridge that the father of my friend Anthony Laughton had said to me quoting from his own experience that through cricket and music you continued to make worthwhile friendships. It was good advice, and although I was not always in the team, I relished the chance of being on hand in the field where there was always something to do.

A feature of the East Midlands division of the NCB was the employment of former professional cricketers. I met several in my time but the most memorable was Bill Voce. Bill and Harold Larwood were the international bowling partners on the well known Bodyline tour to Australia in 1932/33 When at Area I discovered Bill running the post and mail room which was next to my office. A quiet and self effacing person he used to put his head round the door and we would discuss the latest from Australia and local news. Quite often I would see him shopping accompanying his wife in Nottingham and he was always ready for a chat.

Singing with rugby teams was a feature in my day but it happened later with a difference. Paddy (the Rev) Craig asked me to meet him in church one morning. He had obtained the music of "Ireland's call," the anthem which the team sang before international matches. His idea was to adapt it to "Christian, Christian, standing tall we'll answer Our Lords call" Would I sing it with him as a duet in Church next Sunday. He had a strong voice, but one never knew on which note he would start. However after the first go we have sung it together several times at the beginning of services and it is a rousing statement of faith which our congregation seemed to like. It is one of the best of the Rugby anthems and I always join in.

CHAPTER 14

"City of London remains as it is..."
Joseph Chamberlain 1904

It was in 1980 that with IEA splitting up and David Broadbent retiring, that I opted for a post in the Pension Funds. I was therefore introduced to the City, as it was called, and the world outside coal_and thus a number of new colleagues and contacts. The Funds, there were two, Staff and Mineworkers, but combined for investment purposes, were run by three Welshmen, all different in their ways and all of whom went on to other institutions in the City. Sir David Prosser became the chairman of Legal and general, Lionel Anthony a fellow musician, ran his own company Causeway and eventually went to Brussels, and Hugh Jenkins, who masterminded the development of the Funds, went to Prudential. The whole outfit was answerable to Brian Harrison whom I had known since Mansfield days, and we eventually some 25 years later ended up together as members of the court of the Worshipful Company of Fuellers, another City institution, where he was notable for raising funds in the City for charity

I arrived at a time when exchange controls had been lifted and the Fund, under Lionel, was developing its venture capital arm, going into American property, Lemon groves, Farming, films and eventually the Watergate Building. The Fund had about £1 million a day to invest, and the formula was 30% stocks, 30% property, 30% fixed interest with 10% in cash, but the Trustees would adjust this according to the market. I was given a portfolio of tasks with both the property and the investment sides, in-house insurance and administrative functions such a budget, publicity and new staff. This was not always easy as the Coal Board was based on staff grades and the City on performance and bonus. Rules on foreign travel were restrictive and investment staff needed to travel at the drop of a hat. There was also the spectre of Arthur Scargil,1 who questioned all investments if they were not located in mining districts and interfered with some of his more respected Union Trustees. We ran two funds, one for staff and one for mineworkers, each having its own Trustees and administrative arm for the distribution of pensions. I made good friends with many of the property surveyors and it was good to further the career of Alison Hayes who had been with me at IEA Coal and found her feet with the building surveyors, being by family a city person. Being located in the city was an experience and during this time there was a royal wedding and thanksgiving after the Falklands war at St Pauls just up the road._The office moved from the old Punch building in Bouverie Street to Cavendish Square a flagship building of the fund but not without a certain difficulty with the parent board of the Coal Board,which was vacating space at Hobart House and needed to make good the overhead. None the less the Funds are still in Cavendish Square but under a different name. There is no doubt that this scheme was of its kind a remarkable achievement, and well managed and controlled by people respected in the City before the days of tighter regulation and the change in tax.

Although sadly not allowed to contribute to investment, I did manage to introduce an opportunity to the scheme to an opportunity which was a success. This came by chance when Peter Parker invited me to the preview of a film on the famous Scottish rail line to Fortwilliam. At lunch I met John Chittock, who was then film critic to the Financial Times. He told me about some entrepreneurs who had got together with Robin Scott of the BBC and were recording opera productions from existing footage with a view to creating a market for home viewing of opera. I was obviously intrigued and reported the idea to Lionel Anthony, whose department were already investing in films. He must have given me authority, because I found myself being invited to showings and eventually organised for his people to meet up, the investment was made and more films of opera at Covent Garden with Domingo and other artists went ahead, to which I was fortunate to be invited. The scheme was in a consortium to spread the risk and eventually the company was able to stand on its own feet and our pension fund was the richer, thanks to my being in the right place at the right time.

At this time I got to know Michael Murray a silversmith by trade, who was concerned by the lack of accommodation for craftsmen like_himself, in the centre of London. He managed to obtain sponsorship from Legal and General, for converting a hospital in Hackney as workshops for entrepreneurs. Thinking that I had influence, he asked me to be a Trustee along with the chief executive of L&G Joe Palmer, and so I began to learn about the use of redundant buildings for smaller and emerging companies sharing services such as conference rooms, secretaries, reception and of course security. Several others were in this field including Gillian Harwood, a neighbour and friend of Miles. Through all this I met Frank Welsh, who, after a career in industry and as an author, which he is still today, had devoted his time to a non profit industrial property association in the north of England. Frank's company eventually bought out the Hackney property so Michael capitalised on his effort and set up something for his retirement. I went on to meet Frank when I went to Business in the Community (BIC), and others such a Sir Ernest Hall whose complex in Halifax provided both employment and educational.

In 1984 Dick Bresland offered me a secondment to Business in the Community (BIC), and suggested that I met Stephen O'Brien who was the Chief Executive. It transpired that he was at his home with a leg problem, but his secretary, Sarah Darling, suggested that I travel down to his home in Surrey, where I was picked up by one of his sons and taken to meet him. Stephen had been a money broker, had been ordained as a priest in the Church of England, and had attempted to enter politics. His large family, some adopted, gave him that air of compassionate idealism, particularly with the ethnic community in London. The talk went similarly to that with David Broadbent, and he said quite soon what are you doing next week? He wanted me to attend a special meeting of many of the people who supported BIC as it was then known and put a toe in the water. There were three elements to this. First, the great and the good of politics, Lord Carr and of Industry Alistair Pilkington; second the middle aged managers, in which group I belonged, characterised by Ralph Spreckley and Christopher Norman Butler; the third the rising generation of competent social operators such as the late Robert Davies, and Cathy Ashton a CND activist, now Baroness Ashton. To this mixture was added a number of secondments from the Civil Service from Under Secretary John Jardine and other senior officers. The trick was to release government money for creating

76

employment and induce the private sector to do their bit in matching resources; we were each given specific roles in the process.

Both Ralph and Christopher and their wives remained friends. Christopher was a former President of the Union at Cambridge, related to the Butlers and a Private Banker. He had remarkable nerve and an infectious sense of humour. Having no children, he and Annie entertained lavishly in their flat in Ashley Gardens, where one met politicians, clergy from London and artists in a round of introductions, which left one spellbound. Christopher was a specialist on military history and battles. One morning someone in our open plan office asked how to spell Culloden, (it may have been the crossword) and Christopher launched into a description of the battle which kept us going for half an hour. His great coup was a conference in London of both British and European industrialists and once again I called on the underutilized services of Hobart House. Vicomte D'Avignon and Lord Robert Carr were joint hosts at the reception at Goldsmiths Hall with Christopher, a grand finale for him. Christopher Thackeray Norman Butler died in Brussels in 1994 but Annie is still in touch. Ralph after quietly and efficiently seeing the Prince of Wales Business Forum effectively launched, supported and set on its course under Robert Davies, left for retirement in his beloved Hampshire. Ralph, who came from a brewing family in Worcester, had a sense of the ridiculous and patience which was essential in BIC, where it was necessary to leave what ego you had acquired elsewhere at the door. Those who didn't usually ended up by not fitting in or being ridiculed. I only once saw Ralph get really annoyed and that was with Lord Robert Carr. Laughter was never far away when in his company. All this was at a time when his unmarried daughter was expecting twins. Another of that ilk was Alan Dow who, after sixteen years as Personnel Director of London Electricity, excelled at getting companies to second executives and was universally liked and respected. Older than most of us he was a very wise colleague. We both ended up with houses in France. Somehow this crucible, where people came and went and where everyone was very busy, located, as we were in an open plan office discussing and freely inventing ways of doing things and getting money worked. We were all at the end of our careers or in the case of younger ones not sure where to go next, but we made it happen and that quite quickly. A notable of the younger generation was Robert Davies, a maverick workaholic, with experience as a social worker, a local councillor for Labour, who was able to charm company chairmen and chief executives, who came running to the party, particularly when Prince Charles was there. His early death was a tragedy to the movement. This was our means of funding what we did and the partnership worked well. I remember no less a person as John Quinton, the chief executive of Barclays Bank attending our start the week meeting on Monday mornings

So began government industry partnerships with Manpower services, Home Office, Rural Development and anyone who wanted to join in. Most of our works was in fixing deals in the community. One learnt how to be an enabler and to network. One did not force the pace, one waited and draw together those who mattered. This meant that I might be called upon to chair a meeting or speak when others might have been too partisan. I had to make my case at Board meetings or with interviews with senior executives or company chairmen. One might be called in to pull people together or be the expert witness, as in the case of getting underwriting for insurers in unsatisfactory conditions. One was an expert in the subject, and could turn up at a moment's notice to represent BIC whether appropriate or not, but one was expected to be there whether at weekends, or late evenings whenever the busy world was hushed and it was time to talk about social responsibility, duty to the community, ways and means, secondment, volunteering. A ruse towards the end was to make us account managers for companies, which I and others did in addition to having a region to look after.

One got handed anything which seemed appropriate. I had an assignment to meet Sam Wananmaker who was starting to build the Globe and we ended up having a beer together. An insurance broker from Lloyd,s Charles Robbins, a Middlesex cricketer wanted to do his bit by making insurance easy for those starting enterprises in high risk inner city areas. I was summoned to appear before a group of underwriters in their lunch hour to explain what it was all about and then it took off.

I was given a project to start but insisted on having a secondee. Two arrived in turn Chris Simpson and Rani King to write about life after redundancy, and it was a shock for them to become accustomed to the informality and free for all of our office but they were both very capable in their way. Rani became a close friend and we still have many laughs as I try and keep up with her progress to day in the Civil Service. Another was Sophie Marzan, a half French half American girl who came on secondment from a management college and looked at European initiatives.

In addition to my London duties where I had my desk I was Regional Director for East Anglia which consisted of Norfolk, Suffolk, Cambridge and Essex, contrasting environments with differing solutions. For example we had the fens around Wisbech which was a depressed part of England because it was between the science parks of Cambridge and the new development of Peterborough. There was a forward thinking officer in the local authority, Dick Laurie, who grasped the nettle and together we were able to wheedle a number of counsellors and advisors sponsored by their employers to move about and improve business in the fens. There was Jack Scown and John Mawer who took to this well.

We transported this into Norfolk where the circumstances differed as larger firms were closing for economic reasons and smaller businesses were expanding and needed the non executive director type to help. We acquired a very senior manager from Norwich and a financial Director, Denis Crome who became my deputy. Denis was Norwich through and through, very loyal and not interested in London where his future might have been on takeover. We had a common interest in choral singing and Suzanne and I spent some time with him and his wife Bernice when Denis was in the choir singing an all night vigil piece by John Taverner. Norwich was a family run town, the Colmans, Gurneys and of course the Norwich Union, the centre piece of the city. They were good contacts for me and I lunched in that great dining hall or in private dining rooms. The guiding light was the flamboyant director of the Chamber of Commerce, Alex Miller Brown, who guided me through the politics, and who introduced me to the Jarolds and others. Then there were the surrounding areas of Great Yarmouth and Kings Lynn. The latter was a fiefdom for

Sir Jeremy Bagge BT, and several of the farming community who had close contact with the family at Sandringham. I did get a visit there when Prince Charles had a reception for one of his charities, the Youth Business Trust and I remember the cobwebs and mosquitoes in the main hall. Great Yarmouth had its own politics and Birdseye Foods, while Lowestoft, bordering on the broads, had Shell, the training of personnel for the off shore oil, and a gas terminal at Bacton.

It was because of this that we wondered whether there was an affinity with the Grampian initiative in Aberdeen, so we arranged to take a party up to Scotland to learn from it. For transport we acquired the Whitbread private plane, which I boarded in Middlesex and we picked up the others in Norwich, before going on to Aberdeen. We were entertained well by Shell and the locals, and it was an opportunity to put Great Yarmouth and Norwich people together in one environment to get them singing from the same hymn sheet. Whether it worked ultimately I don't know, but it was a good thing for Business in the Community to bring people together to learn something from another's experience and I enjoyed the trip back from Norwich solo with the pilot and his deputy.

The raison d'être for all this were the enterprise agencies, following the example of Pilkington's at St Helens and well described in the book "Pathfinder, The origins of the Enterprise Agency in Britain" by Ian Hamilton Fazey of the Financial Times . Business in the community took over the running of these until they were able to form their own organisation. My task was to help get them secondees as directors, and sponsorship which was then matched by the government. I visited the agencies regularly and we arranged to train the staff at Durham University Business School where Professor Alan Gibb became the guru. Some of them could aspire to becoming training organisations in their own right with contracts from the Manpower Services. This was the time of cutting down the State and offloading as much to other and more local services, which ended up with the setting of the Training and Enterprise Councils which were to occupy much of my time before I retired and to give me further years consultancy with Essex after I retired. This included being on hand for visits from government ministers such as Tim Eggar, John Cope and David Curry. In the early days it was David Trippie, a North Country Tory. Our local MPs were also good at turning up when we needed them. There was Anthony Grant in South Cambridge, Tony Newton in Braintree, Malcolm Moss in the Fens and Bernard Braine with whom I had a meeting on Canvey Island with all the community interests to prevent yet another enterprise agency being set up.

An excellent example of this was David Grayson, from a younger generation than us, who after an industrial career set his mind to finding business opportunities for younger people in the North East. He and his colleague related well to this age group and to the skills to which they could aspire such as fashion, hairdressing as well as the conventional service and manufacturing. David eventually joined BIC and his energy and vision led this movement becoming more professional, self regulating and with its own charter of proficienc. This separated the sheep from the goats, and prevented the muddle which might have arisen, had it gone unchecked.

We also had close connections with charities, including the Prince's Trust. I was pleased to be around for the start up of Emmaus, an initiative for supporting and solving the problems of the many homeless, which was imported from France and had its first settlement in Cambridge, not far from the St John's Innovation Centre, who provided an office for their organiser Jane Burton. I had seen the settlements in France and when planning permission was being sought I rang up a friendly counsellor and asked her to help its approval through. I am told it got through by one vote, but today the charity, headed by Terry Waite, boasts many settlements and I still see Jane who is their principal fund raiser

It was towards the end of the 80s that Prince Charles became President of BIC and we first lined up to meet him at a session in Lloyds Bank Headquarters. Stephen O'Brien had engineered this well and he was quite firm in trying to make his time with us interesting and imaginative for him and not just another royal chore and handshaking. This involved having his equerries attend our directors meetings to get the flavour of planning, and as some of these turned out to be secondees from industry, we had something in common. I worked on two royal visits, attended Highgrove on two occasions and was pleased to have him visit the St John's Innovation Centre in Cambridge where we started a project to take out innovative ideas into local business. For this we got two high powered secondees from ICI and TI, funded by the DTI in Cambridge, during Michael Heseltine's push for new technology when he was Secretary of State. Working alongside my King's friend Eric Howells, who was the University Industry Liaison Director. We brought is a variety of people and interests. It was difficult to estimate what had been achieved, but it got people together and spread such funds as were available for innovation.

Among the Prince's interests was architecture. Charles Knevitt, architectural correspondent of the Time, persuaded the then editor Charles Douglas Home, to sponsor an award. It was based on the community architecture vogue which was bottoms up and letting communities decide their own environment instead of being in the hands of short term and remote planners. I had seen something of this when Robert Davies sent me on a day out with a community architect in Southampton working with pieces of string on a plan. I was asked to become an ajudicator on the Times scheme, the chairman being Rod Hackney, a community architect. Others were Sarah Hogg, then on the Times, Sheila McKecknie of Shelter, Sir Andrew Darbyshire and others. Charles and I became good friends and when he found himself extracted from the Times on the assurance of Rod Hackney that the prince was going to establish a new and bigger charity, he became footloose and we managed to get him a corner at BIC. Charles and I went to Northern Ireland, Derry/City where we met Paddy Doherty, an entrepreneur for all time with IRA connections but a builder, rebuilding his city with positive and practical ideas to take its people away from destruction and give them a new horizon. We had to give the award to Paddy in the first year and he met the Prince, who could not visit Derry, although they got on like a house on fire. Charles Douglas Home ran this from his wheel chair until he died and attracted the great such as Lord Scarman and Wynford Vaughan Thomas. We ran for about four years and his widow Jessica joined us. The trouble was Hackney who talked big about the Prince, but when it came to the crunch, the Prince's Charity Committee just froze him out. I was sorry for Charles Knevitt, who was a distinguished writer in his own right. We worked on several things together and he had a happy marriage with Lesley one of the girls of BITC, as it then became known.

In 1990 when I was about to be 60 British Coal, as it had become, offered me a redundancy package and the start of my pension. I was encouraged to take the package as the terms might not be available later. This should have been the end of my secondment but BITC asked me to stay on and pay me the top up of my salary. This seemed attractive and I was grateful to the powers that be, as I was over retirement age. Two years later they suggested that I should wind down by doing fewer days and handing over some of my responsibilities to the up and coming generation. A new team was taking over and the secondees from business were getting younger. Perhaps on reflection I should have left sooner like Peter Janes, Christopher and Ralph and started NHS or consultancy sooner. As it was I cleared my desk finally before Christmas in 1993, had a party with the family at an art gallery in Albemarle Street where daughter Felicity exhibited, and left to do my jury service in Maidstone when the New Year started.

Not that my work in the community had finished, as in addition to an appointment as a non executive director of the Weald of Kent NHS Community Trust, I had been offered consultancy by the Essex Training and Enterprise Council. I had the task of upgrading some of their action plans, using my knowledge to explore their potential for the future, retaining my contacts in this field and keeping in touch with East Anglia, BITC and the world from which I had retired. This was useful experience and I learnt to work on my own, meet deadlines, and even get some response from the private sector which they were a bit slow at doing effectively. I became Shillingford Associates and had to file my return, pay my insurance and so Suzanne and I were for a time running our own businesses from the same house and same computer. This consultancy lasted for the whole of 1994 and by then I had heard about British Executive Service Overseas (BESO) which begins my chapter on Volunteering.

The quotation from Joseph Chamberlain, with which I began this chapter, was from a speech he made at the Guildhall extolling the City as the Clearing House of the World in 1904. During the ten years of my time there, from 1984 to1994 I had seen the same institutions adapt and had met those who ran them, as they found roles for themselves in the changing environment of the late 20th century. I learnt to mix with royalty, politicians, industrialists and others, and above all not to be overawed.

CHAPTER 15

Volunteering

My time at Business in the Community, made me aware of the amount of volunteering which went on in our society. I had always been aware of VSO through Deborah and her son Tom. Secondment had taught me that I had something to offer and had given me confidence to work in other fields. So when British Executive Overseas (BESO) came along I had no hesitation accepting their offer and was excited to be travelling overseas as my father and mother had done in their working lives. Our first BESO assignment was to Bangladesh in 1995, to the renowned International Centre for Diarrhoea Diseases Research, (ICDDR, B) dealing mainly with children under five, suffering from severe dehydration. The situation was horrific, queues of dehydrated children at the gate each day, mothers searching for comfort and doctors being needed to fulfil demands, some of which were quite basic deficiencies in health and nutrition knowledge. On average the hospital treated one hundred thousand patients a year, but more when there were floods or epidemics. They paid a generous tribute to me in their journal saying that I "suggested ways to reduce the cost of patient care and improve financial management to provide treatment to an additional 1,500 patients a month" (GLIMPSE Vol 19 3 September 1997 ISSN 0253-7508). There was a need to identify cost information by disease episodes and to account for all clinical function. Dr M A Salam and I discovered that short term treatment was considerably cheap and effective, less than 5 dollars a patient, so they were able to concentrate on the more serious cases where the fatalities might occurr. This also helped separate clinical from research cases where there was a lot of cross subsidy, and show just how much was needed to treat an epidemic when it happened. This was my first venture and achievement in the humanitarian field and it was merely applying common sense and management ideas to a situation which was becoming out of control. They were very polite and complementary and I was invited back on two further occasions to emphasise and develop this work.

It takes a long journey to visit third world, a long journey and I was keen to prove what I could do. At this time John Harvey Jones, formerly from ICI was doing his trouble shooting series on TV and I found his methods and approach very useful in the assignments which I took on. I tried to approach them with an open mind and to evaluate them in the context in which I found them which could be very different in each case.

The first assignment to ICDDR, B in Dhaka as described above, was one of the two best things which I had done in my life. I met some great people in Bangladesh, Asem and Loretta Ansari who were most hospitable, and Graham Wright, a trained accountant who organised the assignment, and went on to an important job in the Department of International Development. BESO paid their tribute to me and gave me star treatment with a special certificate and an invitation to an evening party at Buckingham Palace attended by all the members of the Royal Family

There was another side to this. Suzanne came with me and although she at first saw it as a bystander, having coffee mornings with other expatriates, we soon realised that we could work as a team. We had always worked in different fields, she with her business and I with mine meeting in the evening to discuss our day. Now we were a team complementing our skills and when we went to downtown hospital in Assam, this transformation began to bear fruit. We went back there again twice and our diaries are witness of what we did and how we helped create something special. The tasks were not difficult compared with the politics and pressure of our professional lives. Somehow we had found something in our sixties which we could offer. I think that Edward and Marianne found this early in life and that is what makes them a great couple. In our generation it came later but it was none the less important as cement in our lives. Our life with the Dutta family and all their friends was very rewarding and we learned to love India.

Our diaries in India and Nepal are a living record of this and a story of service at a time when many couples might be taking to the golf course or becoming SAGA holiday louts. We did have our excursions to Delhi Agra, Taj Mahal, Jaipur. Chitwan, Katmanhu and Kasaringa. We saw game parks and rhinos, palaces and temples, museums and local craft industries. We brought back rugs and other artefacts. In addition we met the Dutta family, Reeta and Mahesh in Nepal, Raqib and Nafisa and so many others who have became our friends.

We were able to offer our flat in London to Chabbi Gaudel when he studied at the Institute of Child health. When we offered it, we did not anticipate that the course would last a whole year, so we made a more substantial contribution than we had expected. We set up a charity for ICDDR, B in the UK and have had lots of contact with Istiaque Zaman on his visits to the UK to raise awareness of their work among the British Bangladeshi community.

Our sixties were an important and rewarding part of our lives, frustrating yes but also surprising in results and fun. Don't write off the troisieme age if you can still do something which excites and adds to your experience of people and life.

I wasn't really sure where I was going when I landed in Dhaka Bangladesh in October 1994. After a stop at Dubai airport, a revelation in itself, I found myself at ICDDR,B as it was known. This hospital, described by Andrew Tomkins as the only place in the Third World where western scientists can work with their counterparts of the Third World, had been established in 1975 not long after the secession of Bangladesh from Pakistan. The Centre was run by an Ethiopian Paediatrician Demisse Habte, a cheerful, bubbly kind of person, at home wherever he was in the world, a great mixer in diplomatic circles and for ever building support for the institution and himself a great partygiver. I was put up at the guest house, an air conditioned assembly of rooms and corridors in Gulshan a residential area of Dhaka, looked after by stewards who gave us meals and washed our clothes. A car called daily to take me to Mokali where this cholera hospital, as it was known was situated. I made friends quickly with the home team, particularly Graham Wright, to whom I was assigned and Patrick Vaughan, later to be joined by his wife Pauline whose daughter Sarah was to become the wife of the future Prime minister Gordon Brown. There were also Nafisa and Raqib Anwar, British Bangladeshis, who had come to try and put something back into their home country as many of the bright academics of Bangladesh working elsewhere did, but sadly politics were against it.

I spent three separate assignments to ICDDR, B but my first was the longest lasting up until Christmas and during which I worked hard and achieved something for which I am proud but didn't realise it at the time. The hospital statistics showed in graph form the number of patients being treated and they were pleased to be reaching over 100,000 a year. The finance and accountancy branch was showing an ever increasing cost and contribution to cover this. The donors wanted value for money, and the research programmes were quite happy to experiment on patients without having to cover the cost of treatment. I came up with a revised information system which commenced in 1996 which was quite normal accountancy in costing out everything as and when it was done. The savings were some 10%. As the bulk of the patients were short stay, the cost of this was less than a dollar and, as we identified the longer stay patients, we could see which were subject to specialised treatment, which were subject to research and above all where the mortality cases occurred. They said that this reduced child mortality, and they gave me credit for this.

In all I had three visits to ICDDR, B and made good friends. I went back in the monsoon season in 1995 to present my ideas to the Trustees. It was a very friendly time. I fitted in a visit to the special surveillance area in Matlab and tried to do a similar exercise for Patrick Vaughan, as I had done for the main hosptal. He was responsible for this part of the enterprise. Loretta and Asem Ansari were hospitable hosts at their house in Gulshan. Their son Sanjay later visited us in London and we took him sightseeing to Lloyds and the Bank of England. I also found time then to pay my first visit to Calcutta, unfortunately spoilt by an attack of really bad diarrhoea, which made me realise what we were trying to cure in young children. I was entertained well in Dhaka, as indeed we had been on the first visit, when the British High commissioner had asked us to several functions and we moved around the diplomatic circles. It was on this occasion that I met my old chum of the LPC Dick Davis from Chicago, whom I ran into at the American Club after attending church with some American and Ethiopian friends.

Our next assignment was to Guwahati in Assam where we were to be at a general hospital called downtown. We arrived in October 1996 and were greeted at the airport with Assamese red and white cotton scarves hung around our necks; Suzanne was given a bouquet of flowers and we were ushered off to a hotel by the Brahmaputra River. We were the guests of Dr and Mrs Dutta. This part of our life is well chronicled by Suzanne who kept a daily diary as she was to do for all our future assignments. This assignment was a happy one, as we had a great rapport with the Dutta family and their friends in Rotary. The Duttas were a remarkable family; he had qualified as an ENT surgeon in England and Bordeaux and she taught at Cotton College, the university in Guwahati, as well as supervising the domestic arrangements at the hospital. His style included inviting nursing recruits to sing a song from their native area at their interview. On a walkabout he stopped to admonish his well qualified and comely receptionists about treating their counter as the Laksmi line (the line in India lore which you were forbidden to cross for fear of evil spirits) and exhorting them to move out among the waiting clients. We found the staff at the hospital easy to get on with and although we worked six days a week, they found time for us to visit the game park at Kazaringa and took us to Shillong for the weekend. This place still had something of the British hill station about it. We stayed at the old club for expatriates, where the sheets, although linen, were well darned.

During our visit Suzanne was able to prepare all I needed to show statistically on the computer, much to the surprise of the office staff, whose own system was subject to failure. She was asked to speak at a press conference on how she saw Guwahati and some of the journalists present asked permission to print it in the local papers. She had described the traffic chaos at crossroad, where all vehicles inched forward in advance of the policeman's baton. Her diary indicates the busy social whirl which we had with speeches to Rotary, the Management Institute, which was included as a contribution in their journal, as is the custom in Indian society where there is much emphasis on the written word. I also lectured to the university staff standing for over an hour in tremendous heat.

Before our second trip in 1999, I had been given a Rotary International Volunteer award, which I subsequently received from the UK national President of Britain and Ireland. I wrote the following:

"What *are* we doing here? I thought. Suzanne and I were on our way to work. It was the middle of March and we had made the same journey for six weeks already, six days a week, starting at eight in the morning and finishing around five in the afternoon. We were in North East India; it was hot, the temperature would be in the thirties and, as there had been no rain five months, dust was swirling in front of us in the early morning haze. Sweepers at the side of the road were enveloped in their own little dust storm, and it was difficult to see where they would dispose of such dust piles as they collected.

We were on a voluntary assignment at two hospitals in Guwahati, Assam. We had completed four weeks at the Neurological Hospital and were now at downtown General Hospital, the visits being arranged by BESO and supported with a Volunteer Grant by Rotary Foundation, as I belonged to the Rotary Club of East Grinstead in Sussex.

My overall task at downtown was to help the hospital attain a set quality standard and Dr Dutta, the managing director and himself a former District Governor of Rotary, had suggested that I take this forward by meeting each head of department at the hospital, at a rate of four each day to thrash out their individual draft for the quality manual being created. We had been given a suite of rooms on the sixth floor to carry out these interviews. My first appointment of the day was at eight thirty, so long as the Indian indifference to time keeping allowed! Suzanne was with me, making a note of all the suggestions. We were both over retirement age, have a 17th century house on the Kent-Sussex borders, a holiday house in South West France, children and grand children to watch growing up. However we need to be up and doing and so had chosen to come to Assam on this nine-week assignment.

Progress could be slow and to illustrate the reason, I will take you briefly through a typical day. My first appointment was with the Chief Storekeeper. He was worried that he couldn't write a quality manual, and started to explain why. We adjourned to his office to see how things stood. The small room was crowded with cartons waiting to be unpacked, and the shelves stacked with everything from aspirins to stethoscopes. 'Just explain what happens' I said and we started to look at goods received notes etc. A bright looking Indian clerk was posting entries into a computer, but there was also a large leather bound ledger book. 'Why a double entry?' For problems with quantities and discrepancies. I looked at the manager who had been assigned to me they started to speak together in Assamese which, of course, I couldn't understand. After each burst, he would speak to me in English, in a way which I knew meant that his mind was working out a new method to save time and effort. The computer man smiled at me, glad to find that he had an ally. We talked about the system and how many more variables we might add. He showed me how he could create a print-out showing individual expiry date for medicines. The debate went on, while at the other end of the room nurses were queuing at a window for prescription medicines, rather startled by the presence of the foreign gentleman involving himself in their daily routine.

Next I went to patient records. Two rooms of stacked papers, where an operator on an old word processor was copying doctor's notes and adding to daily records. Why did the back room have to be different and muddled? Why the records could not be taken direct from the computer entry already started in Reception, which was peopled with charming girls dressed in blue and moving around with lightning efficiency. (An important part of their job specification was that they should smile at patients and put them at their ease). We could cut out duplication and save some space that could be used by the Micro Biology Department, where patients had blood specimens taken over the same counter side by side receptionists entering records. Not very hygienic you may think and I agree. Healthcare might be a high risk business by our standards, yet this hospital had been identified by Times of India as being at the cutting edge of treatment and had carried out a successful brain tumour operation by laser on a twelve year old within the last few days.

In the afternoon I had two appointments with the medical staff from the Operating Theatre and Chest Pain Centre, a new venture to distinguish heart problems from other respiratory problems. Sometime would I look at the proposals for a new hospital and medical school out of town in a tribal area? Was there a chance of European funding for this?

The situation in India is vastly different from that in the West, with waiting lists post code lottery etc. Expectancy and access to healthcare are low, but there are no waiting lists. North East India has the lowest number of hospital beds per head of the population and the highest number of unattended births. Private and public medicine is blurred, everyone pays something at the point of need, but talents tend to be centred in the urban rather than the tribal areas. Yet the standards of the medical practitioners were as good as you could find anywhere and they were up to date in what they offered. They were prepared to work all hours and weekends if there were patients waiting, and many came from other provinces, on their own initiative, with family and could not be turned away until diagnosis was carried out. One wondered about the others who didn't make it and were left in ignorance of the cures available. To move out to tribal areas, even with clinics and mobile teams, was a humanitarian necessity but how to make it sustainable was the question that exercised the entrepreneurial Dr Dutta.

I have quote the activity of one particular day, and at the end of it there was a delay with our transport,so we didn't leave the hospital until after 5 PM. There was just time for a short rest before speaking to one of the three Rotary clubs of Guwahati. I was considered instant-speaker material, capable, they assumed, of giving a measured comment on any subject they chose. I had already spoken to one Rotary Club on World Peace and the Vice Chancellor of Guwahati University had invited me to give a talk on Management in Higher Education. On one occasion, the chairman said, that as Suzanne had never made a speech, perhaps she would now like to come forward and tell the meeting about British reaction to the death of Princess Diana. No warning and a possible minefield. As visitors to this State capital, a city of some 20 million, we were significant strangers and made welcome by all sorts of people, including the politicians.

How did I get involved initially? In about 1993 I put my name forward to BESO and, because I had been a non executive director of a Health Trust, I was asked to visit hospitals in the third world. My knowledge of health was obtained by reading papers, attending board meetings and conference, but occasionally one was given freedom to break loose and talk to the professionals in their departments on a one to one basis. I remember that my chairman in the sixties liked to see all his unit managers once a year on their own for one hour and this was to me a key management factor.

Back now to India and the end of five weeks' work on the Quality Manual. Due to the usual delays we were unable to take it as far as I had hoped. My frustration and restlessness were beginning to show. Suzanne spent her time editing syntax. It was a dilemma for us, trying to hold a balance between the English and the Indian use of the English language. Meetings could not be held because of holidays, bereavement or, quite simply, people just not turning up!

The last day saw a farewell laid on especially for us. They spoke in turn in tribute "We didn't feel you were strangers" they said "but part of the hospital family" as they called it. "It was good that you shared our interest in cricket" (I had been invited to umpire a cricket match with another hospital), and 'beloved sir' although you were cross with us you always had a smile. We were showered with gifts and, as our vehicle drove us away through the muddle of rickshaws, motor bikes, cycles, lorries and buses, we felt quite tearful thinking of those wonderfully warm people who, are so attractive, because, despite all the drawbacks seem to rise above it with an air of constant optimism.

Will you be back again soon Sir, Madam please? We looked at each other and could not fail to say YES OF COURSE."

We were there from 16th January to 18th March, working hard at two hospitals, but being entertained and occupied all hours of the day. Suzanne's diary is a chronicle of customs and idiosyncrasies but it shows that we were really in love with life in Assam and relished the time and the work despite frustrations. The time was memorable for both of us, giving us a worthwhile job, a chance to sample local food and buy silks and other things which took our fancy. Our houses bear mementos of Assam; the Duttas, their family and the other doctors became our friends, with whom we have lasting links. Riti, their daughter, came to Birmingham to study hospital management and stayed with us for the weekend, and her parents occupied our flat in London while on a special visit. It seems that we made helpful contributions to the two hospitals, the Neurological Research Centre and downtown, run by dedicated clinicians, Borah a diligent practitioner and Dutta more convivial and a networker, both equally effective in designing centres of clinical excellence, through their own efforts. Writing in 2007 Ramachandra Guha in his book on Democracy in India said that doctors born and trained in Assam went on to establish clinics in Bombay, but these two stayed to improve the health of their own people.

In between the Assam Visits we were in Nepal at the Christian mission hospital Green Pastures in Pokhara run by International Nepal fellowship (INF). We first went to Nepal in October 1998, flying via Doha and Kathmandu. We had the opportunity of an early holiday at Tiger Mountain village, near Pokhara where we did some tentative trekking, nature observation, and visited remote villages during a festive holiday. We also saw Tibetan culture, their monks and prayer wheels in the Tibetan village set up by refugees from that country. INF was originally leprosy focussed but was now branching into spinal injuries, education and social work. My assignment to the Release Project was with leprosy patients, their recovery, rehabilitation and skills which included farm management. The mission expatriate group came from many countries, Germany, Finland and Holland in the main, but also some from the Commonwealth. The Nepali staffs were partly Christian part Hindu and kept themselves separate in hours of work and worship pattern. This land locked country had not only its currency but its own unique calendar and months of the year. We found this strange. We were faced with a number of projects masterminded by committed Christian expatriates, who had short duration secondments, and a central office which was mainly Nepali but operated at a distance. It was a dilemma of whether to strengthen the centre or go for self supporting units. I went for the building up of the professional capabilities in the centre and leaving the projects to concentrate on their specialities, without getting bogged down over administration. I advocated flatter lines of_command, and centralising such local talent as we had, to work for the whole. As there was a plan to relocate the central office on the site of the Green Pastures hospital and its surroundings, it seemed a natural development, but several did not like having their local teams disbanded. It was a new experience to have my presentation for a business meeting prefaced with a bible study from Timothy, but I managed to finish my remarks with a quotation from Philippians. This fusion of Christianity with business worried Suzanne, but we both got the hang of it in the end. We learnt more about the style of the Christianity as practiced very openly, a combination of evangelical C of E and openly declaimed non Episcopal practice.

It was during this assignment that Suzanne was given her own work to do, training secretaries and creating forms for new and emerging projects to do with HIV, and drug addiction, funded by United nations and the European Commission. Wim van Brakel presented her with a cloth and napkins embroidered by the occupants of the Rhabilitation Centre, before she left. We both worked quite hard but had time for relaxation at Lakeside, and among the Annapurna range of mountains which we viewed from our sparse guest house room at all hours of day and night.

We were very much left to ourselves and had little social contact with the other members of the mission other than at work. Part of this was due to the fact that Wim Van Brakel who was in charge of the project was away a lot. He was a distinguished epidemiologist and eventually ended up in a senior post in Delhi. He was very supportive of my suggestions and I pointed out that I was surprised at the low ratio of Nepali staff employed in proportion to the number of ex patriates. One of the problems was that they only promoted Christians, but Wim took it well and said that perhaps INF should aim at more involvement of Nepalis. I tentatively suggested job sharing when the ex pats went home on leave. I had checked out the comparison with the Britain Nepali Trust who operated in the same way in another region. We arrived home in time for Christmas and then we were off to Assam early in the New Year still on medication for malaria.

On our next visit in 2001 we had more social contact and got to know more Nepalis such as Reeta Gurung and her family and Chabbi Gaudel, who had occupied our London flat for three terms while he took a degree at the Institute of Child Health, and had visited our house frequently We had a protracted walk across the mountains of Ananpurna to visit his family, an experience which left us both exhausted. It was almost a trek and needed much stamina. When you got beyond their shyness and fear of how to treat strangers, they were a happy and easily amused people with a great love of dancing. During the second visit we had many fun evenings at the guest house with Nepalis, Laotians, and other nationalities who came to learn the good practices at Green Pastures. This time we met Grace (Amazing Grace) Warren, an upfront Australian with voice as loud as 100 decibels. She made quite certain that her methods were understood. Our task was to look at the various activities of the Green Pastures Hospital, beautifully situated in the footholds of the Annapurna range. It was changing from a leprosy hospital as founded, to include surgery for spinal injuries, developing prosthetic limbs, and a rehabilitation for teaching those affected by such conditions to return to their villages literate and able to cope with their disability. The size of the hospital enabled closer working and involvement of both Nepalis and ex patriate missionaries. The dedicated Finnish family Jukka and Piera lived on the site, bringing up their family as did his predecessor Friedbert Hermm, a musical German doctor. We tried hard to change things for them and standardise ways of working. Sometimes it worked but it was a slow and uphill task. After a time the missionaries finished their stint and went back to their own countries.

Our final assignment with Beso was in 2002 and it was mainly Rotary. Nundra Nath Dutta , as we learn to call him, was having the Rotary District Conference at Guwahati and wanted us there, so we persuaded him to find a job for us, and Beso

89

found another for us in Calcutta. I was thrilled with this idea as I had seen Calcutta briefly once before, and wanted to show it to Suzanne. We were given star treatment by the Downtown family, and after the social life at the Rotary Conference at which I had to speak. There were celebrations at Cotton College, the Festival, weddings, so our social life was well catered for, and Suzanne bought herself material for dresses from the lovely Assamese silks and enjoyed the company of the Indian women whom we met. I was invited by Dr Dutta to speak to all the doctors and find out how they viewed their employment and the way in which the hospital paid their remuneration. He thought that they might be more open with me. This went well and I came up with an idea suggested by one of the senior doctors but it wasn't really to his liking. We left after ceremonious farewells, in song and speech, making us feel what a warm, expressive and outgoing people these Assamese were, and how Dutta's imagination and intuition for management had given downtown a unique approach as to what a hospital should be. I remember being fascinated by his approach, as typified in the poster on the wall at the entrance to downtown and which read as follows;-

"A patient is the most important visitor on our premises.
He is not dependent on us. We are dependent on him.
He is not an interruption to our work. He is the purpose of it.
He is not an outsider to our business. He is part of it.
We are not doing him a favour by serving him.
He is doing us a favour by giving us an opportunity to do so"
                    A statement attributed to Mahatma Ghandi

We left in mid January for Calcutta and sadly this was not to be a very satisfactory close to this occasion. There were difficulties over accommodation, and we found ourselves having meetings at city clubs with formal and well dressed Indian gentlemen, or meeting people from institutions such as the chamber of trade or Rotary Clubs without seeing the knitty gritty which we believed we had come to see. In all we managed to see two Calcutta people projects, a mental health one by accident, and the other that undertaken by the Rotary Club of Calcutta at Bishnapur, a memorable enterprise by the first Rotary club of Asia with a membership of 300. Socially we saw the cricket ground, Mother Teresa's Convent, the markets and the Cathedral, not forgetting a special evening with our friend Lalli Crow from England who just happened to be there.

The interest in Rotary is very great on the subcontinent with new clubs being formed and meetings taking place at weekends. They make ambitious pledges of money, great undertakings by Rotoract and other groups for clean water, developing economic activity etc. Formality is significant, as in the west. Every meeting began with the singing of their national anthem. At one meeting in Calcutta Suzanne and I were invited to follow this by singing our national anthem. Two voices competing in a silent and crowded room. We have continued to be amused by the experience.

This is the end of a long chapter which Suzanne has chronicled day by day. Why did we finish? I was 71 and Suzanne was 68 and we were both finding the six day working week, ten week stints, the lack of home comforts and how to keep healthy, problems which were difficult to manage. Our recovery time on return was getting longer and we were more vulnerable as travellers. We appreciated the chance to see new cultures, contribute something of our talents, and the warm and continuing friendships which we made with those with whom we worked. Our forays as tourists whetted our appetite for more and they are a source of enjoyment in our memory. Volunteering accounts for another one million jobs, the Princess Royal said. It was an experience for both of us. Twice in my life I have been invited to a garden party at Buckingham Palace and through volunteering I had another opportunity to attend an evening party with all the members of the Royal Family and many others who are engaged in charity work. It was a privilege to be included with so many people from this field of activity.

All this was great fun and we found ourselves undertaking things which we would never have believed we had the confidence to do. We took part in the opening of an Enterprise Fair in Guwahati and during that week seemed to be seen on television every evening. I was asked to give a lecture on management and this was reprinted in the journal. I used analogies from cricket, the orchestra, flexible home working, and team building. Suzanne gave a talk on promotional gifts and the need to keep up quality and adhere to deadlines. In Guwahati we had our private armed guards to look after us everywhere we went, including at cricket matches, where I umpired games, gave commentaries, presented man of the match awards, all faithfully recorded in the papers. In Calcutta together we sang our national anthem to a meeting of a Rotary Club, and spoke at a Rotary District Conference attended by Rotarians from the Bengal district. It is a chapter in our lives which we look back on with great delight at all we were able to do at that time. It goes on to this day. Iwas delighted recently, when Patrick Vaughan invited me to a reception for the Bangladeshi Regional Arts and Crafts at Downing Street when his family were there, where I again met cheerful smiling people from that country who continues to have environmental problems but somehow overcome them. And it has to be said that they are improving on the cricket field.

CHAPTER 16

Chasing one's tail

Joining a NHS Trust board as a non executive director in 1993 was a new experience for me. The internal market for health was a policy of the 1990s and up and down the country, the NHS became more commercial and accountable. This led to all sorts of anomalies and rivalries creeping in such as beauty contests for logos. Llawyers, accountants and insurers were also there to pitch for business, so many people got rich on this and there were meetings and lunches. Journalists wrote it all up and there was plenty to swell our brief cases with more reading.

Whether the patient got any more out of it as we chased around trying to find who should pay if someone from Devon had a road accident in Tunbridge Wells, we shall never know. In addition to sitting at board meetings and asking questions, we got round the clinics in our area which offered anything from chiropody to birth control advice. A lot of this seemed a waste of money, when we knew that physiotherapy was in demand and the supply was being met from private practice.

There was conflict with general practice about the decision to cut down on the matron and equivalent role, so that we had senior and experienced staff in their cars for half the day or on the telephone. A Human Resources Department was set up with all the professional paraphernalia of records and computers but it seemed that all this went on at a distance from the point of treatment. There was an exception. The St John's Clinic in Sevenoaks under Dr Andrew Wilski, a Polish psychiatrist, built up a rapport with both health and social works in tackling mental health. This became the pattern for the organisation of mental health psychology and for those who wanted to drop in and talk to staff.

My time as a non executive director of the weald of Kent Trust was from 1994 to 1997 but I continued with the Trusts in Kent as they amalgamated and, on leaving, was retained as a Mental Health Act manager. Eventually in my late seventies, I went on to do similar work in Surrey and Borders. The objective was to provide services for all types of mental illness, but resources were few and the government kept changing the Act and complicating the issues.

In 2006 I was asked to do more work in Mental health when one of our administrators from Kent , Wilma Turner, went to Surrey and Borders Trust. This I was happy to do and so began a number of appointments on the west side of the M25 as distinct from the Kent side on the east of the county. New legislation on both mental health and mental capacity has taxed our minds as we wrestle with how best to treat and to preserve some form of lifestyle for patients who suffer in this way. Sometimes I take on a double session and can do several sessions a week.

This was the era when Institutions were closed and the less disturbed mental health patients were housed in the community. I found this important and when I took over the similar situation of my mother's cousin Patricia Collen, I was able to learn from some of those who had carried this forward. The large institutions were in forbidding and impractical buildings, where large corridors and wards made it wasteful and expensive on staff. Many had burn out long before retirement. The switch to housing, with domestic and recreation facilities more accessible and intimate, was an improvement opening up new dimensions for the clients and giving more initiative to the carers.

I was able to carry something forward from my time in Business in the Community if only by suggestions. I understood bout the initiative "Investing in people" and suggested that we went for this charter which was a favourite of the then Prime Minister John Major. I also made contact with British Airways and got them to come and talk about customer relations, comparing what they did with hospitals and clinics. We had a half-day presentation and I hope it paid off, but as in most health trusts many of our brighter people moved elsewhere or even went into consultancy.

It was in 1998 in the summer that I persuaded ICDDR, B to let me have Ramzan Ali, their hospital_manager, with whom had worked in Dhaka, for three months shadow training with us. In addition to working with our people, I got him to speak about ICDDR, B and their work to the hospital staff and to meet people such as the Bangladeshi High Commissioner, all of which gave him greater prestige and opportunity when he returned home. He did very well, although he was homesick at times. We made him a surrogate member of the family, as family relationships are very important to the Bangladeshi people. He once asked if there were any tigers in the woods over Sevenoaks. We also arranged for him to see something of Brighton Hospital, which was much larger than any of our own.

At his time I was becoming very health oriented as my volunteering experience with BESO was taking me out of the country and away from the NHS. When the Labour Government came to power in 1997, I found myself being introduced to new ministers at BESO and as a non executive director to the new Health Secretary, Frank Dobson along with other non executive directors to see how the present system worked and avoiding making unnecessary changes and, in the case of BESO, making a case for continued Government support.

I also joined Rotary, inspired by what I had seen in India, and attended the club at East Grinstead. It is a small club, but offers good company for both of us. I had hoped to do more but my impact has been modest. It has given me the opportunity to have reciprocal membership at Villeneuve sur Lot, so when in France I join them for their meetings, which are of a different variety, but amusing nevertheless. Through Rotary we met John and Jill Ferry, who share many of our interests and are very good friends to us, welcoming us when we arrive and are a source of contact when we are not in France. In 2009 we enjoyed a trip to Brussels, Lille and Bruges with this club and found them very convivial and good company.

Writing now in, we can evaluate something which started in 1986 when we purchased a derelict barn in the Lot et Garonne in South West France. We had been going abroad on self catering holidays and thought that it might be a possibility for retirement. Gigouzac was a hamlet of disused farm buildings and we acquired our barn with about two acres of land for £5000, a ridiculous price. The story of the building is not without incident and problems, but now we take time out to spend most of the summer, enjoying reading, relaxation and a social life of a different kind. We have music nearby, and neighbours and friends on hand when we need them. We have had family and friends here and enjoy showing them the countryside. Although up to 2008 our time at Gigouzac was limited, due to our working at Glyndebourne during the season, we feel part of the scene having been here since 1986. We have restored and built up our garden and house, making decisions and choices as we go along, a process we enjoy.

Now that BESO assignments are no more, and since retirement we have time to enjoy our life at Cowden. London is within easy reach, and local friends and interests to fill our time. I discovered that there was a Livery Company, the Fuellers, of which a number of my former colleagues from the Coal board were members and we have enjoyed the social and ceremonial occasions which this brings. I became a liveryman and a member of the Cour and joined the General purposes Committee. Not having been Master, I have now reached my sell by date as a Court Assistant but they have kindly elected me to the Honorary Court.

Community life in both Cowden and Gigouzac has led to an expanding a circle of local friends, some of whom become closer as one gets to know them. Bernard Burdock is a case in point. A shadowy figure of the village, he was inherently kind and took in much of what went on around him. Sadly missed I see myself becoming more in his mould as the ages of our neighbours around us in the village become younger. I am now Vice President of the Village Cricket Club and of Hartfield Club as well. I am not all that a regular at the Fountain pub, as was Bernard, whom we got to know well; he had great depth, savoir faire and judgement, if rather short of luck and resources. He loved cricket and church so he was a needed ally in the village. At his funeral the church was overflowing. Kim and Joan Baker ran the Crown when we came to Cowden, and we got to know them and their children as they grew up. Their hospitality has continued in retirement and we have many good evenings together. They have stayed with us in France.

The parish at Coleman's Hatch has been a source of friendship and fellowship for about twenty years. Paddy Craig has departed but Nicholas Leviseur, a contemporary of Simon and Charles at Oxford, is our Non stipendiary. How he juggles with his life as a barrister worries me, but his approach to ministry brings him closer to my generation and he has similar inclinations about worship than many older than he. Another friend is Caroline Keddie, as she was when we first met her, but now married to Antoni Daszweski. Their life and interest in travel and opera , together with all the contacts which they make are companions with whom we spend much enjoyable time. Although things at Church have been less happy since Paddy left, we have progressed the music, and I seem to take services regularly, and take funerals, particularly of those whom I have visited. We have established a circle of parishioners who meet on Thursdays at what we call "Time Out." It is a chance to open the church, gossip, discuss matters of interest and pray together. Geoffrey Ogle and Trish Gray and Caroline have helped carried this forward.

My sermons and other writings are all retained and I treasure the first one which I gave on Christmas Day 1994 to a congregation that included the late Lord Hailsham, whose daughter Mary lived in the parish. I had just returned from

Bangladesh and my text was "And the shepherds returned, glorifying God for all the things that they had heard and seen;"   I then described what I had seen of mothers and babies who suffered in the crowded hospital in Dhaka,(see 15) and equated that with come and see the wonder of the nativity and how we, who visited Bangladesh, offered above all our concern with the conditions which, as with the magi, was appreciated.

I find that I have also written pieces for Church magazines on Easter Music quoting George Herbert about whom I did preach in 2008 so he must be very much in my subconscious as I develop my own feelings for ministry and respect for what we have inherited and continue to love in the Anglican tradition. I try not to teach, but to share as a lay person what the faith has meant to me with pointers on how we might do better.

I have called this "Chasing One's Tail." T.S. Eliot said "in my end is my beginning" and since "Walking with Kings" we have travelled far. Yet as an animal chases its tail, it may because it has nothing better to do, or it is amazed how long it is! I won't comment further. So much of what I do now conforms to what I have always done, church, sport and fellowship with others. If I add travel and what I have seen in India and elsewhere, the horizons have broadened and this continues. Suzanne says I am happiest when networking. With the close family around for my 80th birthday and the following weekend in Ireland with my cousins, this has been a time for revisiting that network. Only connect as, Morgan Forster said, and I believe the connection is oneself and what one puts into life makes that connection.

Gigouzac 2010

Epilogue

Most of this has been written during 2009/10 when I had both time and space at Gigouzac for what was a recall from memory. It was during 2010 that questions were asked about my becoming eighty in October and how this might be celebrated. Despite nervousness about this event, I fell in with the idea of a family party but the dilemma was to decide where and for whom.

At about this time, my cousin Anthony Shillington discovered the date of my birthday on the family tree and suggested that we should meet and record my recollections of the family and he would as it were interview me. This led to a session in a studio and then many additions of periods of my life, music and recollections of family homes, holidays and anecdotes. He had also studied the history of the family before my grandfather David Graham so was able to talk about this as we traced our heritage.

The party was eventually held at Gigouzac, the criteria being those of whose upbringing I had been a part or whom I had held in my arms as babies, as well as their other halves. Some 25 came and despite industrial action by the French traffic controllers, they were assembled for the Saturday and we had an enjoyable day. There was time on Sunday to invite our friends and neighbours to join us and for a time the weather was kind to us. It was a very memorable occasion

2010 was a year of interest in Portadown where the Shillington family had come from in Ireland. Because 1860 had seen a revival of Christianity and the founding of the Thomas Street Methodist church, by our ancestor Thomas Averell, we were invited for a week end for the 150th year celebration and a chance to discover more about our family background. This happened to be the weekend after my birthday in October and it was attended by all my cousins and some of their children as well.

It all began with a dinner at the Royal Belfast golf Club organised by my cousin Kenneth Wheeler. The occasion was also his and Gloria's golden wedding. Anthony had already produced copies of the DVD but we used the evening to celebrate both occasions and let our hair down with some of the action songs which we used to sing at Christmas as children.

The following day saw us in Portadown visiting the family shop adjacent to the saw mills where I remember my grandfather taking me as a boy, and it was my first experience of industry. We walked to the river wharf where the barges used to come up and unload. After lunch we visited the church at Drumcree to see the graves and the font at which I had been christened on St Andrew's day in 1930. We looked at the grave of the Rev Francis Hallahan who was the Vicar then and the entry of my baptism and that of my sister Paula,

With us was Jim Lyttle a Portadown photographer who became a friend with common interest in Windsor Castle, and who along with the Rockhapper Studios and Anthony's skills at presentation did much to enlarge the scope of the DVD and give me some memorable photographs at Drumcree.

In the evening there was to be a concert and not to be outdone my cousin Eve had got some of us together to sing as the Shillington choir along with the other items on the programme. We decided to commemorate the Wesleys, Charles and Samuel by singing "O thou who camest from above" and "Lead me Lord" with me singing the solo! Edward and Marianne who were with us for the occasion joined the choir together with Deborah, Mark,Anthony,Alan, Grania Carol, and of course Suzanne. The large church was packed and we came back for more worship at the service on Sunday morning and there was some sadness when the weekend finished after lunch on Sunday.

The occasion gave me a sense of uplift and a discovery of the steadfastness and faith of the family during those years as they built up their business and proclaimed their faith in music and worship.

The End

Made in the USA
Charleston, SC
11 December 2014